"Too many books are being written to promote the latest fad or method. This is not one of them. In *Making Disciples Across Cultures*, Charlie Davis makes a practical and compelling case for how to live and lead in the center of biblical tension. This book was written out of the wellspring of experience and is filled with real-life stories that bring the principles to life. I highly commend it to you."

Steve Moore, president, Missio Nexus

"*Discipleship* is one of those terms used a lot among Christians but often with little understanding. Ask twenty believers to define it and you'll get twenty different answers. Dr. Charles Davis does the body of Christ a favor by clearly laying out universal principles for growing as disciples and in turn making true disciples. God is calling his body to return to true discipleship and disciple making, not according to what culture dictates, but what the Bible reveals about moving toward spiritual maturity. *Making Disciples Across Cultures* is a helpful and provoking resource for every prospective and current message bearer. Overcoming many false assumptions about discipleship, the church and our calling in reaching others, Davis calls us back to Jesus himself and to each other. The book distinctly reminds us of the crucial component of the communal body of Christ in becoming and making true disciples. I highly commend this encouraging book to you."

Ryan Shaw, international lead facilitator, Student Volunteer Movement 2, author of *Spiritual Equipping for Mission*

"Drawing on his experience as a sojourner in Pakistan and Venezuela as well as his time with TEAM, Charlie Davis shares ten principles that will help us rebalance our understanding and praxis of being vibrant disciple-making communities with God-sized kingdom agendas. You have asked the questions, felt the frustrations and wondered why the Christian enterprise—as so many of us know it—is not working well. Charlie provides transcultural and universally applicable insights to help recalibrate authentic disciple making in your context. Don't be surprised if you and your discipleship cohort are inadvertently reenergized as you get a fresh glimpse of the Holy Spirit at work in and through ordinary people like you and me. An essential read for every individual or group committed to genuine disciple making both in the West and around the globe."

Matthew Philip, director of global outreach, Trinity Church, Lansing, Michigan

"This refreshing new look at the central mandate of missions—making disciples of the nations—masterfully weaves biblical teaching with stories and anecdotes from a veteran mission leader who is both well traveled and well informed. Over his long career in missions, Charlie has seen it all, and his creative 'slider switches' analogy helps the reader put disciple making in balanced perspective."

Marvin Newell, senior vice president, Missio Nexus

MAKING
DISCIPLES

ACROSS
CULTURES

Missional Principles for a Diverse World

Charles A. Davis

IVP Books

An imprint of InterVarsity Press
Downers Grove, Illinois

InterVarsity Press
P.O. Box 1400, Downers Grove, IL 60515-1426
ivpress.com
email@ivpress.com

InterVarsity Press® is the book-publishing division of InterVarsity Christian Fellowship/USA®, a movement of students and faculty active on campus at hundreds of universities, colleges and schools of nursing in the United States of America, and a member movement of the International Fellowship of Evangelical Students. For information about local and regional activities, visit intervarsity.org.

All Scripture quotations, unless otherwise indicated, are taken from the New American Standard Bible®, copyright 1960, 1962, 1963, 1968, 1971, 1972, 1973, 1975, 1977, 1995 by The Lockman Foundation. Used by permission.

While the stories in this book are true, some names and identifying information may have been changed to protect the privacy of individuals.

Cover design: Cindy Kiple
Interior design: Beth McGill
Images: Abstract painting: © soleg/Fotolia
　　　　Color brush strokes: © Jesse Kunerth/Fotoli
　　　　Sound mixer board: © Grosescu Alberto/Dreamstime.com

ISBN 978-0-8308-3690-1 (print)
ISBN 978-0-8308-9716-2 (digital)

Printed in the United States of America ∞

Library of Congress Cataloging-in-Publication Data
A catalog record for this book is available from the Library of Congress.

P	21	20	19	18	17	16	15	14	13	12	11	10	9	8	7	6	5	4	3	2	1
Y	32	31	30	29	28	27	26	25	24	23	22	21	20	19	18	17	16	15			

To all those men and women who

courageously and sacrificially cross cultural boundaries

to make disciples of Jesus—apostles all!

Contents

Preface

The Evangelical Alliance Mission (TEAM) is associated with approximately twenty-five hundred churches in North America and thousands more in thirty-five countries around the globe. Some of these churches are brimming with spiritual vigor and growth, sending out workers near and far to carry the good news. Many, sadly, seem to be retreating from global involvement. Some have stopped growing altogether.

In late 2010 and early 2011, TEAM leadership spent many hours in prayer, fasting and discussion, asking God for clarity on what we might contribute toward renewal, health and global vision in the churches with which God has given us influence. As we prayed, we began to dig down to the level of our assumptions about the church, discipleship and mission. We began to question the models and methods with which we had been operating for decades. As a result of this prayer-soaked process, God revealed to us ten sets of cultural assumptions which were underneath the disciple-making models or methods used by many, if not most, of the churches with which TEAM is associated.

In 2011, through a series of apparently disconnected events, about thirty TEAM leaders and workers in Europe gathered to hear three days of lectures by Alan Hirsch. In preparation for the lectures we read his book *The Forgotten Ways*.[1]

The first afternoon, Hirsch described the need to go down to the level of assumptions, just as we had done, if we wanted to see the fundamental changes necessary for the church of Jesus Christ to grow and thrive. Those of us in leadership who had been asking God for clarity on what needed to be changed were amazed.

It was almost as if our leadership team and Hirsch had been working on two ends of the same puzzle. He was working to bring renewal to the church in the West, examining *theological* assumptions about the church, discipleship and mission. We were working with churches worldwide, examining *cultural* assumptions that influence our notion of the church, discipleship and mission.

As the puzzle came together, a compelling picture emerged, ultimately resulting in this book.

Then we became increasingly aware of many others who were being led in the same direction, not only in the church in the West, but around the globe. From China to England, new disciple-making methods were emerging, built on different assumptions about the church and disciple making.

Many years ago, I began to realize that when we see a confluence of factors which cannot be explained through human reason, we may well be seeing the hand of God actively directing our affairs. As one colleague said, "There is only one Shepherd, and his sheep hear his voice. If we are hearing the Shepherd say something to us, then it is reasonable to expect that he is saying it to other sheep as well."[2]

This book explores ten universal principles of disciple making, focusing on the theological *and* cultural assumptions that invisibly shape how those principles become reality in a wide variety of cultures.

These thoughts are a work in progress. If Jesus is driving this process forward, we will find many others who have heard the Shepherd speaking to them on the same subject, and we will be able to learn from one another. If these thoughts resonate with you, we would love to work together, led by the Holy Spirit.

Besides TEAM leadership and Alan Hirsch, many others have been companions on this journey. Dietrich Gruen, whom I first met at a Perspectives class, almost single-handedly kept me going in the early months of writing, as well as providing the questions for the study guide. Jim Plueddemann, my mentor and friend, constantly challenged my thinking. A task force of TEAM missionaries representing eight diverse cultures on five continents has been testing many of these thoughts. Dozens of authors have encouraged me along the way, and I have tried to give credit to each. InterVarsity Press provided extremely helpful reviews of the original manuscript. My wife, Kris, and daughter, Bethany, gave me confidence to keep going and helped me hone my writing style. Members of my "huddle" have prayed for me. Our longtime friends and partners have faithfully contributed and supported me on the journey. Many thanks to all!

Introduction

My Journey as Disciple and Disciple Maker

I am passionately in love with the body of Christ. That has not always been true.

I grew up in Pakistan, one of three children of missionary parents. After my first grade in the city of Abbottabad (made famous in 2011 by the Navy Seals),[1] the United Presbyterian Mission and The Evangelical Alliance Mission (TEAM) decided to work together to sponsor a school for children of missionaries, called Murree Christian School. Six months of the year, spring and fall, we boarded at an elegant old rest home originally built for English military veterans in the Himalayan foothills. Every school day, we walked a mile from the boarding facility to classes held in a remodeled stone church building built in the Anglican tradition. The three-month break coincided with winter, and during the summer months we lived with our families in rented locations. Against this background, I "became a Christian" at the age of eleven, praying with my mother. I remember the relief I had and the sense that I had joined something big, but I wasn't sure what that was.

PLAYING CHURCH

Those were the days when the movement known as Youth for Christ (YFC) was sweeping the United States with rallies, competitions and choirs. Someone thought it would be a good idea to start a YFC group at our school. We held no rallies, and the exciting sound of the radical singing group, the Spurlos, was not possible, but we were able to plan special youth meetings, led by the youth themselves. When I was in the eighth or ninth grade, I was elected president of the small group of students who had decided to form the YFC society of Murree Christian School.

Our job was to plan a meeting together, but what were we to do? Predictably, we did what we had seen done every Sunday morning: someone read a passage of Scripture, someone picked out hymns from the hymnbook, someone prayed and someone talked about the Scripture. Simple. I had no idea what we were trying to accomplish, or what we expected of God. I have since realized that just like some children "play house," or some "play war," we were "playing church." Somehow we had lost the dynamic character of the YFC movement and were going through the motions.

I remember two impressions from this initial foray into leadership. The first was a vague sense of disillusionment: This is it? No mystery or supernatural power? No hard-won intellectual undertaking like learning French or algebra? No sense of mission to change the world? No. Just put a program together, make assignments and hit the start button. Granted, sometimes following Jesus as his disciples can involve repetitive tasks, and they are not always filled with "shock and awe" in the presence of the Holy Spirit. But at the time, I am not sure if we expected the Holy Spirit to do anything.

The second impression was how easily I could exert control. If I took charge, suggested what we should do and acted as if I were convinced that everyone else would go along, they generally would. I remember experimenting with an authoritarian voice, just to see if others would do what I wanted. Scary. Little did I know how common my experience was. Years later, I asked a new believer in Caracas, Venezuela, how he would describe or define the word *pastor*. Since his previous experience was exclusively in the Catholic Church, his impression of a pastor was by general reputation of the evangelical community. Without hesitation he said, "The one who gets to tell everyone else what to do."

Usually my role in playing church was not as leader, but as passive participant during Sunday church services. My first interest in music began because singing parts with the hymns relieved the monotony of playing church. I would sing melody on the first verse, alto on the second, tenor on the third and bass on the fourth. After we finished singing the hymns, I relieved the monotony by counting rows of bricks in the chapel, studying the support system of the church roof or calculating how long it would be until the sermon was over. I enjoyed the music because I could participate; I never dreamed that it was possible for everyone to be involved in the body of Christ, sharing their gifts with one another. I only dimly recognized the cultural dichotomy between clergy and laity that lay beneath the surface.

Guilt Trips

My parents went on home assignment from Pakistan to the United States just as I was moving into my senior year of high school. My dad had grown up in Michigan, and we returned there. I entered a mainstream high school, joined the YFC group and attended a Baptist church[2] youth group there. My first impressions of playing church were reinforced by two overlapping series of events—helping lead the church youth group, and listening to the pastor become increasingly frustrated with the congregation.

The pastor's wife took charge of the youth group, and she recruited me along with some other young people to form a leadership team. We gathered for our first planning meeting with a few ideas to discuss, but to our dismay and chagrin, we quickly discovered that the purpose of the leadership team was to carry out her mandates. She was in charge of the young people's version of playing church, and she was clearly going to design and run the program.

I wonder now what would have happened to that small group of young leaders if she had taken time to mentor us, discover what our spiritual gifts were and encouraged us to make disciples of one another. Some cultural assumptions were at work, invisible to us. Her understanding of leading and teaching did not include the idea of equipping for ministry.

That disappointing experience combined with increasingly dreary Sunday morning services. For some reason the pastor seemed disillusioned with weaknesses in the congregation and used the pulpit to address the problems by preaching through 1 Corinthians. Perhaps he was obediently doing the will of the Holy Spirit, but what I remember was a long succession of guilt trips, Sunday after Sunday. We were not spiritual enough. We did not confess our sin enough. We did not witness enough. We harbored grudges.

By this time, my parents had returned to their next assignment in Australia, and I lived with my grandmother and attended a community college. One Sunday I was seated in the choir loft when the pastor asked everyone to raise a hand if they had shared the gospel with someone over a certain period of time. I could not remember having shared the gospel, and sitting in the choir loft, visible to everyone, I was overwhelmed with shame, guilt and anger. I did not measure up, and what was more, I was not sure I wanted to measure up. Now I realize that I was deathly tired of playing church properly. Somehow the disciple-making process had been short-circuited.

I had attended church since I was born, made a profession of faith at the age of eleven and by age eighteen had heard approximately 1,800 sermons—counting only two each Sunday. Even though I had experienced some life-changing moments during those eighteen years, not one that I could remember had happened during a church service. I was ready to drop out.

Church of One: Failed Experiment

After my first two years at the community college, I transferred to the University of Michigan, pursuing a degree in music and education. Upon arrival, I decided to look for a church that did not sound like, smell like, feel like or look like the one I had left. I was disappointed. I visited several churches, but something in each of them reminded me of the previous one. Finally, I gave up trying and decided to be my own church. I would simply read my Bible, pray and meditate alone. My father had taught me the doctrine of eternal security, and I reasoned that since I had prayed a prayer and become a Christian, I was eternally secure and did not need to worry about playing church anymore. What's more, I had more time to give myself completely to my study, practice and rehearsals in the music school.

Somehow, even though 44,000 other students were studying on the same campus, I found myself more and more alone. Gradually my spiritual life entered into a long, slow decline. Problems that had never been an issue before began to eat at my soul. Depression and darkness loomed. Loneliness ate like an acid into my being. My suitemates had a stash of *Playboy* magazines, and pornography began to plague me. Friendships eluded me. No matter how much I threw myself into the discipline of making music, practicing my trombone two hours a day for seven days a week, I was unhappy.

I had achieved exactly what I set out to do. With one exception, I was alone. I had fallen into a classic assumption of individualism: that we can be whole individuals, complete and mature, standing on our own two feet. Unfortunately, as later demonstrated in the sociological study *Habits of the Heart*,[3] this assumption is simply not true. Fortunately, God had mercy on me. The exception to my aloneness was a growing relationship with Kris, the woman who would become my wife. She was going to Michigan State University and was my spiritual lifeline.

JESUS MOVEMENT: ALIVE IN THE BODY OF CHRIST

Toward the middle of our senior year in college, Kris invited me to visit a group that was meeting on Thursday nights near the Michigan State campus. The group, birthed through the Jesus Movement, was one of many such groups across the United States, growing amid the chaotic culture of pot, rock music, hippies, antiwar protests, flowers, communes and Volkswagen buses. One Thursday I decided to cut Friday classes, hitchhike the one and a half hours to Michigan State and check out the Thursday night group.

As evening approached, students poured into a living room of a family just off campus. They could hardly wait to get together to sing, share, study and pray. Those that had guitars brought them. Sitting on the floor, clapping to the music, laughing at the stories, admitting to their problems, praying with passion, these people were deeply in love with Jesus. The atmosphere was intoxicating. Worship lasted as long as we wanted, people prayed spontaneously, Scripture and the Holy Spirit guided the discussions. Kris and I felt Jesus wrap his arms around us and lovingly, mysteriously, gently bring us back into the body of Christ. He cleaned me up, melted my hardened heart, set my feet on the Rock and welcomed me to his family.

For the first time in my experience, the organizational structures of playing church melted away from the heat at the heart of the body of Christ. At the time, neither of us was able to discern the reasons that the Jesus Movement so profoundly affected our lives. Was it just that the worship was spontaneous? Was it because no one cared when it ended? Was it because everyone was totally accepted? For the second time I was being touched by a movement, something that scholars are seriously studying today, but all we knew was that we were in love with Jesus again and wanted to follow him with all our hearts.

We were living in a dream. Not only were Kris and I enjoying our first love for each other, we were enthralled with our first love for Jesus. We decided that, if we wanted to make a contribution to the body of Christ, we would have to engage somehow in formal Bible study. We applied to an evangelical seminary in the greater Chicago area and were accepted.

FRIDAY NIGHTS: EXPERIENCING THE BODY

During the first week of seminary, we noticed an announcement pinned to a bulletin board inviting people to an early morning prayer meeting. We wanted to continue what we had experienced on Thursday nights at Michigan State, so we went. About a dozen others showed up that morning, many of us having washed up on the shores of seminary for the same reason: the wave of the Holy Spirit through the Jesus Movement. As we shared our various stories with one another, we realized that we wanted to meet regularly for prayer, worship, study and sharing.

We approached the proper authorities at the seminary to ask for a room that we could use on Friday evenings. Their answer was preceded by a question: Could we guarantee that no one would speak in tongues during our meetings? The church denomination to which the seminary belonged was clarifying their understanding of the doctrine of the Holy Spirit, and they could not afford the possible negative publicity if it were known that some on campus were going beyond the boundaries allowed by their church tradition.

Having been touched by the Holy Spirit through the Jesus Movement, we did not mind how God manifested himself, as we told the authorities. We were denied our request. Instead, we went across the street to the Unitarian Church building. For the next two years on Friday evenings, a group of us met in that building, sitting on the floor, sharing our problems, praying for one another, reading and discussing the Scriptures, worshiping Jesus. We learned how the body of Christ felt, how it grew, what it meant. We did not realize it at the time, but we were making disciples of one another. We had caught enough of the character of the Jesus Movement that we were able to reproduce it, without seminars, appointed clergy or well-designed curricula.

We each attended different church services on Sundays where we carried out our Christian work assignments, but in those settings the opportunity to share our lives deeply with others seemed to happen in spite of the program, not because of it. We met some wonderful people in the church we attended and maintained that friendship for many years, but on Friday nights we learned how to function as the body, inviting the Holy Spirit to minister among us. Something we had experienced in the Jesus Movement was operative in those gatherings on Friday nights but was not present on Sundays. That began a lifelong search—learning how the body of Christ functions at its best.

READY TO TAKE ON THE WORLD—YEAH, RIGHT!

Within a year of finishing up our seminary degrees, our home church, in partnership with TEAM, sent us to start churches in Venezuela. We were full of good ideas. Books like Donald McGavran's *Understanding Church Growth*,[4] Ray Stedman's *Body Life*[5] and Paul Little's *How to Give Away Your Faith*[6] were ringing in our ears. I was prepared to take on the world.

After a couple of intense years of language learning and various transitions, we settled down in earnest to put our ideas to work in a low-income neighborhood of the city of Maracay, Venezuela.

With growing surprise, I began to realize how dramatically different Venezuelan culture was from what I had anticipated, in spite of the specialized courses I had taken on Latin America. My language skills were rising from fair to good, but connecting spiritually was not improving. I would share the gospel in the best way I knew how, but somewhere in the middle of the presentation eyes would glaze over. Even though attendance at our Sunday morning services began to grow, it gradually became apparent that many of my cherished ideas were not going to work. Was it spiritual warfare? Was my preparation inadequate? Was it a lack of spiritual gifting? Or was there something about the culture that was invisibly at work? Something that I did not understand? More and more we began to say, "It's not just that some things are different, *everything* is different." Learning the language was challenging; understanding the culture was daunting!

As I slowly began to adjust ministry to the cultural context, however, I was surprised again by a considerable reaction from seasoned Venezuelan church leaders. Different perspectives on how the church might function were decidedly unwelcome, even ideas that appeared to be more reflective of their own culture.

Now I faced a dilemma for which I was completely unprepared. I was trying desperately to connect with people in a culturally appropriate way, realizing how little I understood in order to accomplish that. At the same time, every move I made to adapt to the culture precipitated a reaction from our Venezuelan church leaders. I was taking a crash course in cultural humility.

Paul Hiebert talks about three broad eras of mission: the colonial, the anticolonial and the global. During the colonial era "missionaries . . . equated Christianity with Western culture, and the West's obvious superiority over other cultures."[7] During the anticolonial era missionaries adopted the "uncritical process in which the good in other cultures was affirmed, but the evil in them was left unchallenged."[8] In the global era, "The gospel calls us all to follow Christ. It also stands in prophetic judgment on all societies and culture. It affirms what is good in each but condemns what is evil."[9]

The colonial era was typified by the statement, "We are right—you need to learn from us." To the extent this attitude prevailed (though there were marvelous exceptions), much of the local culture was abandoned or replaced and the local workers did what the missionaries told them. The anticolonial era flipped this on its head. Now the missionary said, "You are right—we need to learn from you." Everything from the missionary sending culture was suspect, with missionaries doing only what the local leaders told them. The "global era" demands that each culture view itself critically, saying, "We both have something to learn, and we both have something to contribute." The global era demands cultural humility from all parties.

The only problem with this analysis is that it sounds as if there has been a smooth and consistent progression from one era to the next. In actuality, each missionary, no matter what nationality, has to struggle through these so-called eras. Being from a non-Western country does not make one immune to colonial attitudes, and these three eras are often overlaid on one another. Cultural humility is necessary on everyone's part.

What I needed, and what is needed today, is a set of universal disciple-making principles by which to evaluate the cultural and theological assumptions that in turn precipitate the methods and patterns of behavior common in churches and among church leaders.

LOOKING BELOW METHODS

This book is about universal missional principles that need to be true in any culture, even though the methods for achieving them may be vastly different. The book is *not* about disciple-making methods, although it contains many concrete examples.

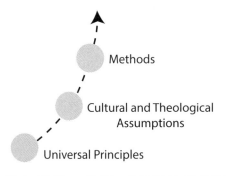

Figure 0.1. Principles and assumptions underlying methods

Missionaries often mix and match methods on a trial and error basis. When something does not work, they read another book and try something else. I did the same. After trying several, cynicism can easily grow, and missionaries can become resistant to the latest bandwagon. The result may be that they find something moderately productive and invoke the need to be faithful, easily becoming trapped in a cycle of ever-lower expectations.

A set of principles helps evaluate any method, allowing mission and church leaders alike to engage in discussion, evaluate various cultural patterns with humility and develop methods appropriate to the culture and capable of bringing those principles to life.

A WORD ON READING THIS BOOK

In this book I use the metaphor of a cultural music mixer board, which deserves a little explanation before diving in.

Imagine a stage with a number of performers, instruments and microphones. You might imagine a massive stage with multiple choirs, orchestra, soloists and conductor. You might imagine an a cappella choir or a worship band. You might imagine a rock group or a symphony orchestra. In the case of a symphony orchestra, the conductor is responsible to balance all of the various voices and instruments, reflecting the proper intent of the music. In many other groups, the sound technician has that responsibility.

The sound technician uses a mixer board rather than a baton. (Ironically, he may not have any training in music!) Mixer boards are large, complex pieces of equipment consisting of multiple slots with sliding switches.

Each of the sliding switches corresponds to a microphone on the platform. One set of switches might be picking up the bass drum on one channel and the snare drum on the other. Another set may be connected to the bass guitar on one channel and the lead guitar on the other. A third set may be connected to the lead vocal on one channel

Figure 0.2. Mixer board

and the secondary vocal on the other. If a switch is set at the bottom of the slot, the corresponding microphone will not be amplified at all. As the switch moves higher on the mixer board, the volume from that particular microphone increases.

When the music starts, the sound technician puts on earphones and listens. If the lead vocal is too soft, he or she increases the volume from that microphone by pushing that switch higher. If the snare drum is too loud, he decreases the volume from that microphone by pushing the corresponding switch lower. If the bass guitar is too soft, she increases the volume on that switch, and so forth. Eventually all of the parts balance, each contributing to the whole but without distortion.

Balancing and rebalancing happens throughout a given piece of music, and the entire mixer board has to be recalibrated with a different type or genre of music. Alvin Slaughter, singing "The Midnight Cry" with the Brooklyn Tabernacle Choir, requires completely different settings than the First Presbyterian Church of Chicago performing Handel's *Messiah*. No single setting is correct for all music, nor will the settings remain constant for one piece of music. The sound technician has to listen continually and adjust the volume among the various microphones. Each style of music demands different settings to showcase dynamic tension.[10]

A church may produce beautiful cultural "music," consistent with Paul's vision of the church, or it may be out of balance, harsh or even discordant. Within minutes of entering the morning worship service of most churches, we gather an impression of their internal cultural music. It may take time to discern what we are hearing, but eventually the impression will become clear. As people within their own culture are less aware of it than the newcomer, so the person participating for the first time will gain a very pronounced awareness of the culture.

If we do not listen closely to the cultural music being produced in our churches and ministries, we will leave the cultural mixer board settings at the same place all the time, losing in the process any sense of movement or dynamic tension. Over time, the cultural music of the church gradually loses the dynamic tension between the various inputs. And if we allow a dichotomist framework to prevail, then we often turn off some of the channels altogether.

At least ten sets of assumptions correspond to the settings that form the cultural music that can be heard in our churches or in our disciple-making efforts today (see table 0.3). Each set is linked to a universal principle for making disciples. Though not an exhaustive list, recalibrating any one of these principles can bring renewal, moving closer to a disciple-making movement.

When we put on the earphones and listen carefully, noticing where we have lost the balance, we can make changes within the activities of the apostolic team or the church to regain our balance and reintroduce the dynamic tension. When we decide to make changes in our activities, the slider switches gradually move up or down.

Table 0.3. Principles for Making Disciples

Principles for Making Disciples	Slider Switches
Disciples Let God Lead from the Invisible World	**Visible/Invisible** To what extent do we live within the parameters of the visible world that we can see, touch, hear, smell and feel? To what extent do we live within the parameters of the invisible world and the rule of God over all?
Disciples Hear and Obey	**Knowledge/Behavior** In the process of making disciples, how much emphasis do leaders give to knowledge transfer and how much to expectations of behavior change or obedience?
Disciples Develop Relational Interdependence	**Individualism/Collectivism** To what extent does the community of believers reflect individualist assumptions? To what extent does it reflect collective assumptions?
Disciples Do What Love Requires	**Gospel-Truth/Works-Justice** Are gospel and works held in tension? Are truth and justice? Or have we settled for one as primary, to the exclusion of the other?
Disciples Make Disciples	**One-Way Delivery/Group Interaction** In the process of making disciples, what kind of balance exists between preaching and interaction between disciples?
Leaders Equip Disciples for Ministry	**Equippers/Ministers** In the community of believers, who is responsible for ministry in the church? Are the leaders actively equipping the people? Or do the people mostly pay and watch others?
Disciples Live an Undivided Life	**Public/Private** To what extent does the cultural music we are producing reflect a division between public or secular and private or sacred domains? To what extent are these lines blurred, with people "living sacredly"?
Disciples Engage in Personal and Cultural Transformation	**Personal/Cultural** In the community of believers, does the church expect transformation and renewal of individuals only at a personal level? Or does it discern and expect transformation of the surrounding culture?
Disciples Keep the End in Mind	**Church/Kingdom** How much emphasis is being given to the church gathered, and how much to kingdom or church on mission?
Disciples Organize Flexibly and Purposefully	**Organizational/Relational** In the community of believers, how much energy and time go toward organizational demands, and how much toward the body within?

I am convinced that many, if not most, disciples who feel they are only playing church are yearning for an experience of the body of Christ as it was designed by God to function, capable of transforming society and redeeming culture. Finding and contributing ways to recover that inheritance is the burden of this book.

SUMMARY

Table 0.3 above lists each principle for making disciples with its corresponding set of cultural assumptions. One chapter is dedicated to each of these universal principles.

What Is a
Disciple Anyway?

Learn from Me, for I am gentle and humble in heart.

MATTHEW 11:29

My wife and I once took a tour promoting a global ministry project sponsored by another organization. After being awed with the interactive displays, the expert use of technology and the global reach of the project, the host informed us, in hushed tones, that for every ten dollars contributed, one hundred people were touched by the ministry. And out of every one hundred people, ten made decisions for Christ. Wow! One dollar a convert. How could it get any better than that?

Coming from the experience of starting two churches in Venezuela, however, I thought of all the difficult moments as we interacted with people who were trying to follow Jesus as his disciples. Each had made a significant decision at some point, but that was only one step of many, involving a lot of messiness and hundreds of difficult decisions and turning points. The cost was immeasurable. How could all of that possibly be reduced to one dollar a convert?

The human building blocks of the body of Christ are his disciples.

How we define a disciple matters. Jesus clearly told his disciples to go out and make more of them. If our mandate is to make more disciples, how do we know when we have succeeded?

I have had several opportunities to teach one of the sessions included in the Perspectives curriculum, the US Center for World Mission's fifteen-week course on global missions designed for church members. On a few such occasions, I gave participants a card and asked them to write a one-sentence definition of the word *disciple*. Of twenty-seven replies, eleven included the word "follower"; other replies included "loves," "learns," "grows," "denies self" or "reproduces." No doubt, all of these can be true of a disciple, but it shows that even among highly motivated church members, we lack consensus on a definition.

Everyone seems to agree that a disciple is not simply a person who prays the prayer of salvation and then goes to a church service on Sundays, although in actual practice this may be the definition that is most common. Churches may be full of people who have prayed a prayer of salvation, but does that make them disciples? Or is there more to it?

Hirsch defines a disciple as "one who follows Jesus and becomes increasingly like him."[1] Bill Hull summarizes a disciple as "a committed follower of Jesus Christ . . . a person who demonstrates belief by action."[2] Others present a combined list of Jesus' statements regarding his expectations of being a disciple, such as denying yourself, taking up your cross, obeying Jesus, loving one another and so forth.

The prayer of salvation may be the first step for many in the journey of a true disciple, but it cannot define a disciple in and of itself. If the body of Christ is going to function as it was designed to function, then any ministry team needs a clear and mutually agreed upon definition of a disciple.

CULTURE INTRUDES

Almost immediately, culture begins to intrude. Just exactly what do we mean by the word *definition*? Cultures categorize things in different ways. Some tend to define things intrinsically, by describing exactly the internal characteristics of the item in question, virtually drawing a clear boundary so that anyone can distinguish between that item and any other. An orange is defined by its size, color, texture, skin, sections, flavor and so forth, so that everyone can tell when they are looking at an orange rather than an apple. Anthropologists use the term *bounded sets* for this cultural tendency to define things by their intrinsic qualities. Bounded sets provide a great deal of clarity, even though it may be misleading: Up or down? In or out? Black or white? Did you or did you not? Categorizing things in bounded sets often leads to dichotomist either-or thinking.[3]

Other cultures tend to define things extrinsically, by their relation to something else. The word *tall* or *short* is an extrinsic definition. My height is six feet two inches. Next to most of my Venezuelan friends, I am tall. If I were in the locker room of the Chicago Bulls basketball team, however, I would be short. Whether tall or short depends on my relationship to those around me. Both descriptions can be true at the same time. This type of definition is called centered sets, and the center is whatever is being compared. Is something ripe or unripe? Close or far away? Happy or sad? If the answer is "It all depends," then the definition is a centered set definition.

A definition for a disciple as one who has "prayed the prayer and goes to church" creates a nicely bounded set. We can easily tell who is "in" and who is "out." A missionary disciple maker can count and report on the number of people who arrive for the service on Sunday morning, or those who have "made decisions" by "praying the prayer of salvation." If any confusion arises, one need only ask the question, "Have you prayed the prayer or not?" Membership in a given congregation is another bounded set category. Are you a member of a congregation or aren't you? If a person can answer yes to these questions, then all is well. Bounded set definitions easily become linked with the idea of goals based on measurable objectives. If you cannot count it, how do you measure it? And if you cannot measure it, why should someone give money toward it?

The extrinsic definitions used by Hirsch or Hull make *disciples* much more difficult to recognize and almost impossible to count. How do we know when someone is becoming "increasingly like Jesus" or is someone who "demonstrates belief by action"? Depending on our cultural background, we may be very frustrated by centered set definitions. Centered set reasoning provides direction and growth, but does not provide much material for measurable objectives. Neither does this reasoning provide the simplistic "punch" favored by fundraisers.

Any ministry team would profit from a thorough discussion of what they mean when they say the word *disciple*. Using primarily centered set reasoning, I want to offer a starting point for that discussion.

Here is a working definition: *A disciple is one who moves closer to Jesus as a learner, follower and lover, together with other disciples.*

Learners

The word *disciple* means learner, and the object of the learning is obviously Jesus. But there is an important difference between learning "about" Jesus and learning "of" or "from" him. Paul said, "You did not learn Christ in this way, if indeed you have heard Him and have been taught in Him, just as truth is in Jesus" (Eph 4:20-21).

"Learn Christ . . . heard Him . . . taught in Him . . . truth is in Jesus." If disciples are only expected to learn about Jesus, then we can satisfy this expectation through the development of discipleship curricula in the hopes that this process will make disciples. Sermon series, workbooks, Sunday school curricula and seminary programs are full of learning about Jesus. Unfortunately, we can learn a tremendous amount about Jesus and still not learn to know him. As James reminds us, the demons know truth about God,[4] and they are not his disciples.

We must also grow in our ability to learn "of" or "from" Jesus, which leads us to actually know him.

Knowing Jesus—not just knowing about Jesus. The Spanish language has two verbs for "knowing." The first verb, *saber*, means to know facts and figures. With regard to Jesus, I can know (*saber*) that he was born in Bethlehem, grew up in Nazareth, died in Jerusalem and was seen alive again by his disciples. The second verb, *conocer*, is to know someone or something experientially. When I meet a person face-to-face and have a personal connection, then I use the verb *conocer*. Or when I visit a city and walk around it, I can use the verb *conocer*. When I say that I know Jesus, I am using the verb *conocer*.

On the last night with his disciples, Jesus prayed, "Now this is eternal life: that they know you [*conocer*], the only true God, and Jesus Christ, whom you have sent" (Jn 17:3 NIV). According to this prayer, the ultimate purpose of existence, now and throughout eternity, is to know the Father and the Son, deeply and intimately.

Paul's first prayer in the book of Ephesians shows how much he desired that the Ephesian disciples would come to know Christ in this way: "that the God of our Lord Jesus Christ, the Father of glory, may give to you a spirit of wisdom and revelation in the knowledge [*conocer*] of him" (Eph 1:17).

Paul believes that "knowledge of him" is the fundamental reality that transforms life and asks that the Ephesian disciples together would be granted "wisdom and revelation" in that knowledge—an intimate, soul-searching, transforming connection with the person of Christ in the context of relationship with other believers.

In another famous letter, this time to the disciples in Corinth, Paul turns his imagination toward the fulfillment of all things at the end of time and says, "Then I will know [*conocer*] fully just as I also have been fully known" (1 Cor 13:12). How well does Jesus know us? Deeply, completely, infinitely. If we keep learning, someday we will know him that well.

The end of the disciple-making journey is to know him as well as he knows us.

Custom fit—not mass-produced. Being disciples of Jesus involves a unique learning process for each person. No two people come to Jesus in precisely the same way. Ask others to tell you of any significant spiritual turning points in their lives, any life-shaping stories. No two are alike. You will be awestruck at the creativity and glory of God. In training sessions for missionaries, I have asked those present to share what they have heard the Lord say to them recently. Each story is unique. Each story demonstrates an authentic moment of growing in faith.

In Caracas, I worked with a group of people who wanted to know how to share their faith with others. I asked participants to find people who had become believers as adults and to ask them two questions: First question: "What do you remember of the content or message at the moment you first believed?" Second question: "What did you feel at that moment in time?"

During the next session, I asked them to report on what they had discovered. Not a single person interviewed could remember the content, or cognitive message, in that first encounter with Christ. All could remember a feeling. Some remembered a sensation of piercing light. Others described feeling deeply loved, or a pervasive sense of peace. These spiritually decisive moments apparently were driven far more by feelings than by a cognitive process.

This was a very limited sample, but it reinforced what I suspected was true. Jesus connects uniquely with each person who comes face-to-face with him in a life-transforming encounter.

I had also stumbled on another way in which culture intrudes into our understanding of the gospel and the unique way each learns of him.[5] Every culture has assumptions about how to determine what is true or not. Some cultures determine what is true by reason and empiricism. People in these cultures amass as many facts as possible, then compare them to one another to determine what is true. They assume that an objective reality exists, and that they can get close to it with enough facts and deductions. In these cultures, emotion is considered a dangerous element that will obscure or twist the findings. The more dispassionate one is, the closer he or she is to the truth.

In other cultures, the truth is determined by the emotion expressed. If someone attempts to persuade others of the truth by neatly lining up all the facts in a dispassionate manner, people will likely believe the truth is being distorted. Life cannot be that simple. I asked an Arab Christian how other Arabs determine what truth is. He replied immediately, "By the degree of passion with which it is spoken." Later, I asked a missionary working in a Muslim context whether this was true among the people with whom he worked. He replied, "Absolutely. Take the common complaint among Muslims that the Bible is full of error because it has been translated so many times. If I argue dispassionately, saying how many texts we have available from the earliest centuries, how closely they agree, how few discrepancies exist and so forth, the Muslim will go away completely unconvinced. If, however, I beat my chest and cry out with shock at the way in which the Muslim has denigrated our holy book and how that hurts my heart, he will stop and wonder if the Bible is true after all." In Western settings, we sometimes see this same cultural contrast play out when a speaker falters for just a few moments, getting choked up. The audience will often respond the same way that the Muslim responds, the emotion confirming the truth of what is being said.

God knows us intimately. He knows exactly when and how to break through into our world. The incarnation continues daily and the learning process for each is unique. Consequently, we cannot mass-produce disciples.

Each disciple is made uniquely, separately, under the watchful eye of God himself.

Lifelong process—not a course. The learning process of becoming a disciple begins long before one understands enough to proclaim him as Lord and continues until we come face-to-face with him and know him as he knows us. Peter and the other apostles were learning of Jesus for well over a year before the spiritual light pierced through the darkness to their hearts and Peter proclaimed Jesus as "the Christ, the Son of the living God" (Mt 16:16). Even then, they had a lot to learn of him before he would be ready to release the future of the redemptive enterprise into their hands and hearts.

I used to believe that the missionary task was divided into three parts: evangelism for the unsaved, a discipleship course for the newly saved and leadership development for leaders. I have since learned that "making disciples" describes a lifelong process. From the first conversation about Jesus with an unbeliever to the final breath, our task is to make disciples—before salvation, after salvation and throughout life.

The process of getting to know my wife began long before we were married, and the process has continued unabated. Even though we have been married over forty years, our relationship continues to grow as our knowledge of each other deepens. That process was punctuated by the significant event of marriage, but that event, in and of itself, was not enough to sustain the marriage. Knowing her, and growing in that knowledge of her, is a lifelong process. So too is the process of learning to know Jesus. It may be punctuated by significant, life-changing moments, but it continues for a lifetime.

Like Christ—not like another disciple. This lifelong process of learning to know Jesus is a journey of becoming more and more like him. No one crosses the finish line in this life. Even Paul continued to strain toward the goal.[6]

Jesus says, "A pupil is not above his teacher; but everyone, after he has been fully trained, will be like his teacher" (Lk 6:40). Jesus is our teacher, and when we become fully trained by him, we will be like him. Unfortunately, it is easy to fall into the trap of thinking that I (the experienced believer) am the disciple-er or teacher, and the new believer is the disciple-ee, my student. If this happens, the new believer, thinking of me as the teacher, will inevitably become more and more like me rather than like Jesus. That would be a tragedy. I am a functional equivalent of the blind leading the blind. "Can the blind lead the blind? Will they not both fall into a pit?" (Lk 6:39 NIV). No human being has the capacity to see what is happening in the soul of another. Only Jesus does. Jesus himself said, "Nor are you to be called instructors, for you have one Instructor, the Messiah" (Mt 23:10 NIV). We must never usurp his role as the Teacher. To "make disciples" means to make disciples of Jesus, not of ourselves. We want others to become more like him, not us.

Culture intrudes again fairly strongly at this point. Some cultures are considered "low power-distance." In these cultures the teacher or leader is a fellow learner who makes suggestions about how to proceed. The distance between the student and the teacher is small, and the teacher might even draw all the students into a circle, identifying with them. Other cultures are considered "high power-distance." In these settings, the teacher or leader retains his distance from the students. He will dress differently, stand in front, often behind a lectern or desk, and dispense knowledge and wisdom. The student is responsible to listen and faithfully reproduce whatever the teacher says. (More on this later.)

In either high or low power-distance, the responsibility of the one teaching is to point to Jesus, not to displace him. This may be harder with high power-distance, but is just as important with low power-distance. In the mutual journey of making disciples of one another, we learn from one another how to be like him. Even the great apostle Paul says, "Follow my example, as I follow the example of Christ" (1 Cor 11:1 NIV). Our task, regardless of cultural background, is to help people see Jesus, so that whether we are there or not, they will be able to continue to imitate him.

To illustrate again using the marriage relationship: The better I know my wife, the more alike we become (with some significant exceptions—I still load the dishwasher in a completely different way). I know what she likes to eat, her favorite colors, books that she likes, preferences in relationships and thoughts about important topics. I know what will please her and what will displease her, and she knows me just as well. Knowing her influences my daily decisions and day-to-day life. It influences my choices of what I do with my time, how I eat my food, what books I read, what clothes I wear. But even in this relationship, there are still mysteries and surprises, even a latent inability to understand and know her completely. But Jesus knows me completely, without any distance or deficit, and someday I will know him just as well. Leaning into that relationship and letting it shape my life, thoughts, actions and character is a lifelong process of learning to know him and to become like him.

This dynamic process of learning "of" Jesus that we have just described leads us to know him and become more like him. Christlikeness is an essential attributes if we are to follow him and carry out his will as his followers.

FOLLOWERS

Following him involves a dynamic process that starts with putting into practice general teachings that he laid out. But it also includes a very specific dimension of doing, saying or going exactly where he is indicating at any moment in time.

As we learn to follow his commands and put them into practice, our lives are conformed to the general truths expressed in what he said. "Therefore be imitators of God, as beloved children" (Eph 5:1). He provides us with many opportunities to love God and those around us no matter how we are treated. The circumstances of our lives give us the choice to seek first the kingdom and avoid running after food and clothing. We learn to trust him when things go wrong or things happen that we do not understand. We become more mature believers by obeying and putting into practice these general commands.

These commands are like the rules of a household: turn out the lights, pick up your clothes, push in your chair, say please and thank you. A child growing up in that household learns these commands, and learns to follow them.

Following Jesus also has a unique dimension. Jesus himself only did and said what the Father told him to say or do, and he expects his followers to do the same. Paul and his companions wanted to go up to Bithynia, but Jesus clearly showed them that he wanted them instead to follow him to Macedonia: "They tried to enter Bithynia, but the Spirit of Jesus would not allow them to" (Acts 16:7 NIV). When Paul wanted to leave Corinth, Jesus told him to remain, because there were still many people in that city who were going to follow him.[7]

In a household, this unique dimension is like asking someone to do something specific: please pick up some bread on your way home; don't forget to call the doctor; can you go upstairs and get my jacket for me?

This specific dimension of obedience often demands sacrifice, but also propels disciples forward. Following Jesus will lead us out into a broken world to convey the Father's love.

Several years ago I heard a Nigerian bishop speak on the version of the Great Commission given at the end of the Gospel of John. After reminding Peter three times to feed his sheep, Jesus says, "You must follow me" (Jn 21:22 NIV). The bishop suggested that the American emphasis on Matthew 28 to "go into all the world" has evolved into a "go-and-fix-it" paradigm, as if we were the ones in the lead, bringing Jesus with us. He admonished us to remember that the great commission in John is the command of Jesus to "follow him" wherever he goes. Jesus is already there, inviting us to follow him, so that he can introduce us to others.

We learn best from Jesus when we follow him wherever he wants to go and do whatever he wants to do, no matter what sacrifice that might demand of us. For Paul, following Jesus repeatedly put him in situations in which he faced suffering and persecution. Many of our brothers and sisters around the world, Afghan, Chinese or Nigerian, to name a few, will readily testify to the cost of following Jesus in obedience.

LOVERS

The true sign that we have been learning from and following after Jesus is this: that we will love like Jesus loved. "By this everyone will know that you are my disciples, if you love one another" (Jn 13:35 NIV). In Ephesians, Paul prays "that you, being rooted and grounded in love, may be able to comprehend with all the saints what is the breadth and length and height and depth, and to know the love of Christ which surpasses knowledge, that you may be filled up to all the fullness of God" (Eph 3:17-19). Love and unity among diverse people is not natural to the human race. Fear, distrust, anger and belligerence are common. When we learn of Jesus and from him while following him, we also learn to love like he loved.

One day, while on our first assignment in Venezuela as dorm parents, I was driving a seven-passenger van full of young people back into the town where the school was located. A storm had passed through shortly before and, as I drove down the main street of town, I noticed a tree branch that had blown down, obstructing the sidewalk. I also noticed a blind old man walking down the sidewalk toward the obstructing branch. I stopped, jumped out, helped the man around the branch and returned to the van. Then I forgot completely about the event. But one of the teenagers in the van did not forget.

During and after college while that young man was trying to find his way, that incident helped prevent him from denying Jesus altogether. He had seen love in action. Only a small incident, so small that I entirely forgot about it until he told me thirty years later. Was I special? No, Jesus had prompted me to stop, get out of the van and follow him over to the blind man. He knew how that seed of love and faith would grow; I did not. I am so grateful that I did not ignore that still small voice prompting me to follow him to love someone I had never met.

TOGETHER

I ran a search program on the Bible for the singular word *disciple*, and then the same search for the plural word *disciples*. With few exceptions I found the word overwhelmingly used in the plural. This should not surprise us. Jesus did not have meetings with each of his disciples separately, lining them up on his Outlook calendar and allotting each thirty minutes in a closed room. The disciples were learning to follow Jesus together, and generally when he spoke, he spoke to all of them. One notable exception to this pattern occurred when Jesus spoke to Peter on the beach after the resurrection,[8] but generally each of them was learning of and from Jesus in a group with other disciples who were also learning of and from him.

If someone famous is in a room and everyone moves closer to him or her, they can't avoid getting closer to each other in the process. The closer they press toward that person, the closer they draw toward each other. In the same way, the closer each of us draws to Jesus, inevitably the closer we draw toward each other. We learn from him together, we follow him together and we love one another together.

WHAT IS A DISCIPLE ANYWAY?

Here again is a working definition:

Learners. Followers. Lovers. Of Jesus. Together.

Learning draws us together into his heart to know him and to become like him.

Following draws us together into his work to obey him no matter what the cost.

Loving draws us into his people, which in turn can transform the world.

Up, out, in.[9] This is what it means to be his disciples, the "living stones" Peter described: "As you come to him, the living Stone—rejected by humans but chosen by God and precious to him—you also, like living stones, are being built into a spiritual house to be a holy priesthood, offering spiritual sacrifices acceptable to God through Jesus Christ" (1 Pet 2:4-5 NIV).

Making disciples takes a lot more investment than one dollar per disciple—it requires everything we have and are.

Disciples Let God Lead from the Invisible World

The Visible and the Invisible

He is the image of the invisible God,
the firstborn of all creation.
For by Him all things were created,
both in the heavens and on earth,
visible and invisible. . . .
He is also head of the body,
the church.

Colossians 1:15-18

At our boarding school in Pakistan, the most popular kids every year were those whose families had just returned from America. They knew all the latest music, games and fashions, gaining instant popularity.

When I started the eighth grade, Sammy,[1] a ninth grader, had just arrived from America. He introduced his roommates to a popular game called a Ouija board. He did not own an official model, but he knew how to make one by arranging letters and numbers on a sheet of cardboard. All they needed for a marker was the cap from a Coke bottle.

Sammy was one of about twenty boys who boarded in half of a single-story duplex. The living-dining area had been turned into a bedroom for seventh and eighth graders, and the three bedrooms housed the older boys, divided by grade levels. In order to get to their rooms, the older boys had to walk through our bedroom.

One night, Sammy and some of his roommates gathered around the board and invited the spirits to answer questions. The spirits obliged. Fear and amazement swept the room. They asked more questions. The bottle cap moved. Brian, one of Sammy's roommates, later told me that they could not lift the bottle cap during the sessions, no matter how hard they pulled. Even after the sessions were over, he sensed the presence of evil spirits crowding around his bed.

Night after night they gathered, terrified but unable to stop. Our school had a strict system of rules, and their fear of punishment equalized their fear of ever deeper involvement with the spirits. They were hooked.

Jason, one of my roommates, was worried about his brother, Barry, who was in the room with Sammy. Barry had told Jason what was happening. One Sunday afternoon my roommates, Jason, Dwight, Judson and I, met to talk about what we should do. We decided we had to tell the principal. With some trepidation, we left the campus without permission, risking punishment ourselves, and hiked to the principal's home a mile away. To our great relief, he listened carefully, took our concern seriously, prayed with us and told us to go back to the dorm. He would meet with the dorm parents, and they would talk to the boys who were involved.

That night the older boys met with the dorm parents after the rest of us had gone to bed. They were ready. They prayed together, claimed salvation through the blood of Jesus, confessed their sin, asked for-giveness and experienced freedom. Fear was gone. Slavery and ad-diction were broken.

That night, in the middle of the night, I awoke to tugging at my arm. Dwight whispered in my ear, "Wake up, Charlie, something funny is happening in our room." As I surfaced, I began to listen. In the middle of the dark room, suspended invisibly about seven feet in the air, I heard a strange mixture of sound like a candy wrapper opening and scratching. The spirits were apparently on their way out, but had stopped in our room. Now we were terrified.

Something invisible was definitely present.

We began to pray earnestly, but nothing changed. The noise con-tinued. Someone suggested we read Scripture, so we fished out our Bibles and flashlights, randomly opening to various passages. Dwight read a psalm. To our amazement, the words seemed to have been written with that moment in mind. As he read, the noise stopped. When he stopped reading, the noise returned. I read an-other psalm, and the noise stopped. I stopped reading, and the noise came back. One after another, around the room, we read until dawn, continually amazed at how the passages we selected, apparently at random, were so appropriate. By morning the spirits had left and did not return.

I learned a profound lesson. The invisible world was real. Evil spirits existed and, if given a chance, would take over. The power of evil was great enough to keep a bottle cap glued to a piece of cardboard, to move in answer to questions and to terrify us with sounds that had no visible origin. But the power of the Holy Spirit was far greater.

The Holy Spirit had the power to prompt words to be written cen-turies earlier that would protect us and comfort us in our hour of need. The Holy Spirit had power to break the slavery of fear. The Holy Spirit was infinitely more powerful than the evil one.

In his mercy, God had led us, motivating us to discuss the situation, guiding us to walk to the principal's home, relieving the fear and addiction of our fellow students and causing our Bibles to open where his Word would be most powerful. We were utterly dependent on him, and he led us out of the trap.

LETTING GOD LEAD CONNECTS THE INVISIBLE TO THE VISIBLE

Letting God lead is one of the most basic disciple-making principles. Some describe this principle as acknowledging Jesus as Lord,[2] others as what it means to be a follower of Jesus. The first time someone explained this principle to me, he showed me a diagram with two circles representing my life. Each circle had a throne in the center and little circles representing various parts of my life arranged around the throne. In the first circle, ego sat on the throne with all the little circles arranged randomly. In the second diagram, Jesus sat on the throne, and all of the little circles acquired order and purpose.

The principle is simple to understand, but fatally easy to ignore.

In order to live out this principle, we need to understand and embrace the healthy tension between the invisible and visible worlds.

Consider the *Sherlock Holmes* thriller produced in 2009.[3] As the story begins, Sherlock runs pell-mell through the dark streets of London in order to arrive before a young woman is murdered in a satanic ritual. The villains of the story are clothed in white peaked hats, evoking revulsion.

Soon signs of the invisible world appear. Someone bursts into flame spontaneously. A dead man comes back to life. Another person mysteriously dies in his bath of no visible cause. Evil is afoot, and Sherlock is in the crosshairs of something bigger than life, something beyond the visible, material world.

In the end, Sherlock reveals, to the relief of the audience, that everything can be explained through natural causes. The person who burst into flames was the victim of a chemical spray. The dead man who walked again had used a special drug that simulated death. A subtly administered poison killed the man who died in the bath. We walk away from the movie satisfied, convinced that those who believe in the invisible world are hapless victims of ignorance and superstition, easily manipulated for political ends.

Sir Arthur Conan Doyle, creator of Sherlock Holmes, wrote his stories during the Age of Reason. The scientific method had developed as the one sure path for discovering truth, ensuring a world under the control of human reason. Rigorous observation and application of the scientific method would guarantee progress for humankind. Scientists began to function as priests; technology, the holy water. All mysteries could be explained with just one more study, one more research project, or by a genius like Sherlock.

And God? A creation of our minds, nothing more. Mysteries and miracles were a sop for those who had not been trained to think or reason properly.

So what are we to believe? Is something else out there or not? Does invisible evil exist? Does invisible good exist? These slider switches of visible and invisible may be the most important of all. Does our work and ministry grow out of the guidance and direction received from the invisible world? Or do we simply give lip service to God and make the majority of our decisions based on demographics, strategy and rational processes?

Sherlock reduces all invisible phenomena to natural, visible causes. My story recognizes the power of invisible evil and the immense power of invisible good. Which story is true? Our lives may depend on the answer.

When the visible slider switch is high and the invisible switch is low, we work primarily with vision, purpose, plans, theories and strategies. We read an endless stream of books that are research-based and completely pragmatic. We pray at the beginning of a meeting and at the end, but invest our human energy in the matter at hand. We respond eagerly to statements that something "doesn't work" or "does work," as if visible results were a guarantee of God's leading. When large numbers of people show up at events, we think that surely what we are doing has God's blessing. In contrast, when thousands were following Jesus, he managed to offend them all so badly they went away.

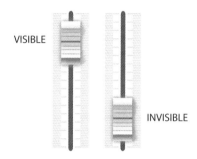

Figure 2.1. Visible high, invisible low

If we set the invisible slider switch high and the visible switch low, however, we can justify anything by saying, "God told me to do this or that." During college, I knew a young woman who was astounded one evening when a man told her that God had told him she was to marry him. That was the first that she had heard of it.

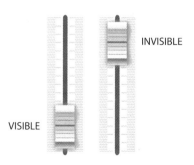

Figure 2.2. Visible low, invisible high

Numerous atrocities can be traced to attributing to God something that he never intended. Saul thought that God had told him to kill as many Jesus followers as possible.[4] Four hundred years of the Inquisition can be traced to a drive to maintain institutional power by claiming divine authority. Jihadists kidnap and dress young people in suicide vests in the name of God. Jim Jones tragically led dozens of people to commit suicide.

How do we reintroduce the tension of living in the visible, material world while remaining sensitive to the power of Christ available to us in the invisible world? How do we know, truly know, "what is the hope of His calling, what are the riches of the glory of His inheritance in the saints, and what is the surpassing greatness of His power toward us who believe" (Eph 1:18-19)? How do we regain the tension between the visible slider switch and the invisible slider switch?

How can we learn to let God lead? How do we teach others to let God lead?

The answer lies in the body of Christ. It forms a direct link between the visible and the invisible. When we carefully submit what we believe we have heard from God to other trusted members of the body of Christ, judging by the Spirit within us and by Scripture, they can help us discern whether what we have heard is indeed from God or if it is simply a product of our own imagination or, worse, if we have been deceived by the enemy.

The visible world has much to offer. Books, articles, education, seminars, ethnographic research and scientific studies all enrich our lives and give us much wisdom. We need to think deeply, study hard and handle facts appropriately. The problem is not that we learn from disciplined study in and of the visible world; rather the problem is that often we have not invested as deeply in understanding and living within the infinite wisdom and incomparable power of the invisible world.

Ruth Haley Barton, president of the Transforming Center, in *Pursuing God's Will Together*, gives a simple definition of the body of

Christ as two or more people who gather around the transforming presence of Christ to discern his will and carry it out.[5] Doing this demands that disciples develop the spiritual disciplines necessary to hear God and let him lead, such as solitude, silence, memorization, meditation, listening, waiting—all disciplines that are in short supply in a busy world driven solely by the visible. A compendium of various spiritual disciplines is also available in the *Spiritual Disciplines Handbook: Practices That Transform Us.*[6] More resources are listed in the study questions for this chapter.

Maintaining Biblical Tension: Visible and Invisible

Jesus Christ is seated in the heavenly places, the invisible world, and all things in that world and in the visible world have been put "in subjection under His feet" (Eph 1:20-23). He commands the "armies of heaven" (Rev 19:14 niv). Jesus calmly tells Pilate that legions of invisible angelic forces are at his call,[7] the same host Elisha called on when surrounded by the army of Syria.[8] God is active in the invisible and visible worlds, and his power is available to accomplish his will. Certainly we need to use all the tools that God has given us in this visible world, studying, thinking, planning and strategizing. Our challenge is to keep living within the dynamic tension where God's work and ours intersect. "Your will be done, on earth [visible] as it is in heaven [invisible]" (Mt 6:10).

Jesus clearly demonstrated that the invisible kingdom had broken in to the visible world. The blind saw, the deaf heard and the dead were raised to life. Despite this evidence, his mother and brothers thought he had lost his mind, his neighbors were offended and the religious rulers wanted to kill him. Some, however, decided to open their eyes, listen intently and turn their hearts toward him. They eventually became channels for the power of the invisible world. Jesus recognized those people as his disciples: "Pointing to his disciples, he said, . . . 'Whoever does the will of my Father in heaven is my brother and sister and mother'" (Mt 12:49-50 NIV). They were learning to let God lead.

Paul uses the term "heavenly places" to describe the invisible world of good and evil, both directly linked to the visible world. Of invisible evil he says, "Our struggle is not against flesh and blood, but against the rulers, against the powers, against the world forces of this darkness, against the spiritual forces of wickedness *in the heavenly places*" (Eph 6:12). Of invisible good Paul says that we have been blessed "with every spiritual blessing *in the heavenly places in Christ*" (Eph 1:3). And referring to the dynamic responsibility of the church to connect the invisible to the visible, he says, "so that the manifold wisdom of God might now be made known through the church to the rulers and the authorities *in the heavenly places*" (Eph 3:10).

Paul was convinced that the source of good and evil was found in the invisible world. Since the body of Christ has been seated with Christ, by the throne of God, it has the power to confront and overcome evil in the invisible as well as the visible world.

That night, huddled with our flashlights reading Scripture together, we were a small example of the body of Christ at work, liberating, protecting, comforting and doing battle. Christ, the source of all power, seated in the heavenly places, with us at his side, confronted the power of evil. Evil didn't stand a chance.

CULTURAL ISSUES: PERCEPTIONS OF REALITY

Finding healthy tension between these two slider switches becomes easier when we work together with people from different cultures as long as the subject is clearly put on the table and debated. I found my own perspective influenced considerably by godly, well-educated Venezuelans who had much greater perception of what was going on in the invisible world.

Research conducted under the direction of Fuller professor Dudley

Woodberry[9] identified six major influences drawing Muslims to Christ, including miracles, healings and visions. Although visions were the least influential of the six, approximately 50 percent of Muslims who had become believers reported seeing a vision of Jesus. One man who had come to Christ in connection with a TEAM missionary was startled when he discovered that the missionary whom he knew had never had a vision of Jesus.

Why do so many Muslims who come to Christ have visions of Jesus, when it seems so rare among Western missionaries? Could it be that Western missionaries have been so influenced by their culture that they have trained their spiritual eyes, ears and hearts not to notice what is going on in the invisible world? If we are going to let God lead, those from a highly rational culture have much to learn from those who have been raised within a culture with a more developed capacity to perceive the invisible world.

One of the most widely read articles by Paul Hiebert is entitled "The Flaw of the Excluded Middle."[10] He describes three levels within culture.

Invisible	God or gods, angels, demons	Other World
Invisible	Leprechauns, fairies, ghosts, goblins, spirits, etc.	This World
Visible	Material matter	This World

Figure 2.3. The flaw of the excluded middle (Hiebert)

The upper level represents both the invisible and the "other world." This level includes cultural notions of God or gods, heaven and hell, angels and demons.

The bottom level represents both the visible and "this world." This level describes the material world—what we can see, touch, smell, hear and taste.

The middle level is invisible, but also part of "this world." This level includes perceptions of leprechauns, fairies, spirits, ghosts, goblins and so on. At this middle level, Africans see evil spirits resident in a tree. Venezuelans perceive the spirits of those who have died, or see rolling balls of fire in the open country that constitute warnings of imminent danger. Indonesians believe that sickness comes from the spirits of their enemies who have died. Americans play the lottery, read and follow horoscopes and wear lucky hats.

Much of the Western world has relegated the upper level to a private and personal "faith space," which is not subject to public debate. And since the middle level is not susceptible to the five senses or the scientific method, Westerners discard it altogether, calling it superstition or "old wives' tales." This "flaw of the excluded middle" opens them to the influence of evil and the evil one, who is prowling "around like a roaring lion, seeking someone to devour" (1 Pet 5:8). The spirits that answered Sammy's invitation were in that middle level, invisible and part of this world. Fortunately, we were prepared enough to find refuge in the Word of God.

The church can easily be overcome with Sherlock's perspective, operating only at the lower level. Church and mission can become solely a matter of strategy and planning, deductive reasoning and logical extension. Demographics rule. Logic wins. We pray, but are we doing battle in the heavenly places? Do we listen enough to let God lead our strategies, or are we building our own strategies, with a quick prayer for God's blessing?

All too often, missionaries move into places in the world where they do not understand the forces of evil at work, nor are they spiritually ready for battle. They may have prepared excellent papers on mission strategy and have professional training in intercultural studies, but are they prepared to deal with the palpable spiritual darkness of a Hindu temple in Kathmandu, or the evil spirits exercising their power in an African village? These are life or death questions.

If that worker goes into these dark places in the world alone, without a team that demonstrates and functions as the body of Christ, he or she will be an easy target for the enemy. The danger of not understanding how to deal with the invisible world will be compounded by the isolation of the worker. The enemy will attack children, health, morals, theology, relationships, integrity and whatever is exposed to his power.

EXAMPLES—LETTING GOD LEAD FROM THE INVISIBLE WORLD

Asking God first. Colleagues of ours, James, and his wife, Ruth, began working in a country in central Asia shortly after the Russians left. Chaos was descending, civil war had erupted and an extremist group was gradually taking over. James and Ruth hardly knew where or how to begin, but they knew of several unproductive methods that they did not want to use. They decided on a simple strategy: pray first, and then do whatever God would tell them to do.

One by one God began opening up opportunities to share the good news of Jesus. One day James heard a knock on the door. A young man was there, asking for a Bible.

Weeks earlier, due to a minor infraction, the young man's father had been apprehended, thrown into prison and beaten. After he was released, he met someone handing out invitations to a cultural event at an English school where the meaning of Christmas would be explained. He attended and heard about the origin of Christmas, the birth of Jesus Christ. The program notes said that he could find the whole story of Jesus in a book called the Bible. He promptly sent his son out to search the bookstores. After some fruitless searching, a bookstore owner told him that he should not be asking openly for that book. The extremist group in power would be ruthless in their punishment. But he told him that down the street and around the corner lived a person who might be able to find him a copy. That person was James. God was clearly leading.

I asked James how he knew whether or not to give a Bible to

someone. He responded that he would look at the eyes. If he saw boldness and eagerness, he would simply feign ignorance and refuse. The person was probably a spy. If he saw fear and nervousness, he would find some pretext to talk to the person again. Then, relying on the Holy Spirit and his prompting, praying with his colleagues, James would eventually give that person a Bible.

James had learned the power of letting God lead. When that young man became a believer, he taught him in turn how to let God lead.

Doing battle in the invisible world. One of the ways to reveal our slider switch settings is to evaluate our prayer life. Are we doing battle in the heavenly places for Christ to overrule the spiritual forces of wickedness, or are we only praying for changes in the visible world, as important or good as those may be? When someone's health is in jeopardy, do we pray for healing—or do we also pray for faith, hope and love from the Holy Spirit to shine into and comfort the person whose health is at stake?

A ministry team is waiting on government permits to begin a project. Do they only pray for the permits? Or do they also pray that in the process of applying, waiting and interacting with government employees that the light and love of Jesus Christ will shine into dark places, exposing any corruption that might be at work (world forces of this darkness) and confronting any evil which might be opposed to them engaging in that project (spiritual forces of wickedness in the heavenly places)?

Another ministry team is trying to break through to their postmodern neighbors in Europe. Do they only pray to meet people and develop friendships? Or do they also pray that the stranglehold of secularism and materialism (world forces of this darkness) will be broken, and that the power of Jesus Christ will defeat the forces of evil at work, forces that through countless religious wars think they have won back Europe for the kingdom of darkness (spiritual forces of wickedness in the heavenly places)?

A ministry team in South Asia seeks ways to be and build the body of Christ among Muslim people. Do they only pray that God will protect them from harm and help them develop the means to win the confidence of their neighbors, leading to the sharing of the gospel? Or do they also pray that the culture of obligatory vengeance (world forces of this darkness) will be replaced with a culture of forgiveness and restitution? Do we pray, as well, against the invisible powers of evil which are enraged at the number of Muslims coming to Christ, that they will be bound and rendered powerless (spiritual forces of wickedness in the heavenly places)?

Everything in the visible world is constanly intersecting with the invisible world. We have been seated with Christ in the heavenly places and have been empowered to call on the triune God for his honor to be upheld, his kingdom to come and his will to be done.

Learning not to underestimate the enemy. An enormous highway runs east to west across the center of the valley in which Caracas lies. High-rise apartments fill the center of the valley, while shanty towns climb up the surrounding hillsides. In the center of the valley, a second highway branches off to the south, connecting the capital with the rest of the country. In the intersection of those two highways, between the eastbound and westbound lanes, stands an enormous statue. The pedestal of the statue rises approximately fifteen feet off the ground, and on top stands a huge stone tapir, similar in shape to a pig but with a long snout. Riding the tapir is the figure of a naked woman, long hair flowing down her back, her arms stretching upward with a woman's pelvis held in both hands above her head. That is María Lionza, goddess of fertility, worshiped by countless people across Venezuela.

Every day that we lived in Caracas, people braved the traffic and delivered wreaths of flowers to this pagan image. Unconfirmed stories circulated that she resided on a certain mountain in Venezuela, served by priests who offered virgins as human sacrifices. According to those we knew in the capital, every president of Venezuela paid homage to

María Lionza in order to acquire spiritual power in the elections.

Was this the reason that our work in Caracas was so difficult, while many other places in Venezuela were experiencing many more people coming to Christ? Was this idolatry part of the reason that so many of our friends and neighbors were blinded to the truth of Jesus Christ? Caracas was the political, economic, artistic and social center of the country. It was not necessary to believe in territorial spirits to realize that some source of spiritual darkness had a hold upon that city. I confess that I did not take it seriously enough. Instead, we relied far too much on our own wisdom and strategic thinking, and not nearly enough on spiritual warfare through prayer and fasting. Our visible slider switch was set high, our invisible slider switch was fairly low.

If I could start over again, we would have regular times of prayer and fasting, calling on God to break the power of evil and to lead us to the key people whom he wanted us to meet. We would have prayed through the Lord's Prayer, phrase by phrase, applying it to people and sections of the city. We would have memorized and prayed the prayers in Ephesians 1 and 3, for his power and love to bring about spiritual breakthroughs. We would have waited together until we were convinced of the next steps that God wanted us to take. We would have looked for spiritual allies within the other churches of the city with whom we could pray together.

Calling on God together. In the year 2000, four TEAM colleagues and I had the privilege of surveying places in Chad where the gospel had not yet been heard. We planned to visit at least one of fifteen small villages clustered around a medium-sized town on the southwest side of Chad where we thought they might welcome a medical clinic. This village of seminomadic Arabic-speaking Muslims was located across the main river that dissects the country, hundreds of miles from the section of the country known for thriving churches among the black African population. Driving over almost trackless scrubland, we arrived in the village early in the afternoon.

Upon arrival, we first spoke to the village elders who were sitting by a wall that functioned as the official village gate. Except for the presence of our Land Cruiser, if Abraham himself had arrived on his camel, he would not have noticed that anything had changed in the world since his time. Electricity and running water were not even remotely possible.

The village chief received us in the official hut just beyond the gate. Led by an experienced missionary, we engaged in an extensive conversation, exploring all possible relational connections. At the appropriate time, we asked if we could drive around the area surrounding the village, as well as spend the night there. The chief graciously invited us to stay the night in the guest area of the village. After leaving his hut, we explored the area, discussing the needs of the village.

That evening we headed to the guest area, only to discover that the original buildings had disintegrated in the sun and rain. The thatched roofs had long ago disappeared, and the mud walls had melted down, serving only to hide people who used them for latrines. Undaunted, we set to work in a nearby area, sweeping the flat ground, rolling out mats and setting up small cookstoves. As we were preparing our meal, a local schoolteacher originally from southern Chad came to greet us. He was a fellow believer in Jesus. After a lengthy conversation, he asked if we knew that the place where we were staying was considered the dwelling of the evil spirits. None of us laughed.

After the schoolteacher left, we held a hearty prayer time, together calling on the power of Jesus for protection. Then we rolled out our sleeping bags and slept under the stars. During the night, many of us woke up to a cacophony of sounds coming from animals nearby. Cows were lowing, dogs barking, donkeys braying, birds clucking and screeching. We never found out exactly what had happened, but it seemed that the spirits who normally stayed in that area had been disturbed, and the animals knew it. Apparently the chief thought he would give us a test, to see if we would be subject to those spirits or not.

Today a missionary team is working out of the nearby town. Gradually, these people are hearing about the good news of the kingdom of Jesus Christ. The team is helping develop wells for irrigation for their fields and giving them the living water of Jesus Christ. God led, and now we are seeing spiritual fruit.

DISCIPLES LET GOD LEAD

God understands all of the complexities of every possible culture. He knows exactly what is necessary for his will to be done, his kingdom to come, his name to be honored. His disciples let God lead. When they do, amazing things happen. Whether you are living in a leafy suburb of America, a big city in China or anywhere in between, let him lead. Teach other disciples to let him lead. God knows what to do.

Disciples
Hear and Obey

Knowledge and Behavior

*For whoever does the will of my father in heaven
is my brother and sister and mother.*

MATTHEW 12:50 NIV

In the fall of 1929, an Indian student named Bakht Singh entered graduate school at the University of Manitoba in Winnipeg, Canada, to study agricultural engineering. By December, the shadow of the Great Depression was spreading throughout North America. Bakht Singh's family in India had also suffered financial setbacks. He was alone, nearly destitute.[1]

During the Christmas holidays, he moved to the local YMCA. On the morning of December 13, in the locker rooms, he noticed a man who appeared happy and asked him the reason. The man replied simply, "Christ in the heart." Owel Hansen demonstrated a joyful spirit that morning, despite the responsibility of managing a bank in the dark days of the Great Depression. He gave Bakht Singh a New Testament.

Three days later, after reading every waking hour, Bakht Singh came face-to-face with Jesus as he meditated on his words, "Verily, verily, I say unto thee, except a man be born again, he cannot see the kingdom of God" (Jn 3:3 KJV). He confessed his sin, and joy flooded his soul. As a Christmas present, Hansen gave him a Bible. Bakht Singh devoured every word. In succeeding days, Hansen introduced Bakht Singh to John Hayward, a Christian businessman. After getting to know one another, John invited Bakht Singh to move in with his family.

We don't know how much fuss or concern Bakht Singh might have caused in Hayward's household as an Indian student in their home. I can imagine that they had many more questions than answers, wondering about sleeping arrangements, food preparation or requirements, gifts at Christmas and much more. We do know that Bakht Singh accepted the invitation, moved in with them, attended church with them, participated in daily family devotions, debated and discussed portions of the Bible with them, and even relocated with them to Vancouver. The Haywards were busy making a disciple. Two years later, Bakht Singh was baptized.

Bakht Singh grew up in the Punjab area of what is now central Pakistan. He came from a devout Hindu family. At birth his mother dedicated him as a Sikh, devoted to the one universal god as a special disciple. When he returned to India in 1933, his mother and father asked him to keep his faith in Jesus quiet, but he responded with the now famous words, "Can I live without breathing?" They disowned him, refusing to let him return to their home. In succeeding years, depending on God for each step of obedience, Bakht Singh eventually began a movement in which tens of thousands of Indians became disciples of Jesus Christ. These disciples would meet in major convocations annually. The convocation in Hyderabad regularly drew 25,000 people. When Bakht Singh died in September of 2000, over 700,000 people visited Hyderabad during the week of his funeral.

Owel Hansen, prompted by the Holy Spirit that December

morning, joyfully shared with Bakht Singh that his faith in Jesus made him happy. John and Edith Hayward obeyed when they heard the "still small voice" of the Holy Spirit prompting them to invite a foreign student into their home. The impact of these simple acts of obedience still reverberates among 1.2 billion people in India and beyond. John Hayward undoubtedly knew what the Bible says about hospitality, and he could probably have quoted passages from Deuteronomy which tell us to love foreigners and strangers.[2] He had theoretical and cognitive knowledge of the Bible. But during the winter of 1929 that knowledge was transformed through obedience. Because of their obedience, Owel Hansen and John and Edith Hayward played an enormous part in changing the world.

Not many will become another Bakht Singh, preaching to hundreds of thousands of people throughout India, but how many of us are willing and ready to carry out a simple act of obedience similar to that of Owel Hansen or John Hayward, overcoming our fears and worries? Imagine being John and Edith Hayward, knowing that their simple act of obedience contributed to this enormous harvest of disciples.

OBEDIENCE MATTERS

Our obedience matters. God is the Alpha and Omega,[3] the Beginning and the End,[4] the First and the Last.[5] He sees the end from the beginning and the beginning from the end.[6] God's purposes span the millennia. We cannot know all the ways in which our obedience will be used in his eternal plans, but he does. We should never underestimate the explosive potential of a single act of obedience to the Holy Spirit, informed by the truth of God's Word.

If we want to be effective at making disciples, then we have to find ways to teach how to hear the Lord and obey him, connecting knowledge with experience, information with action, understanding with behavior. Making these connections does not come naturally; we have to be intentional about doing it.

In this set of cultural slider switches, one switch corresponds to the degree to which one's church or one's ministry team depends on the transmission of information/knowledge to make disciples, and the opposite but yoked switch corresponds to the degree to which the church or ministry team promotes and expects transformed behavior. Both knowledge/information and experience/behavior are important, but if they are not connected by obedience to the will of the "Father who is in heaven," the dynamic tension between them ceases and our capacity and effectiveness at making disciples and carrying out God's will diminishes.

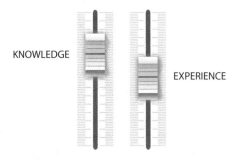

KNOWLEDGE EXPERIENCE

Figure 3.1. Knowledge and experience

MAINTAINING BIBLICAL TENSION: KNOWLEDGE AND EXPERIENCE

When I began seminary, I was required to make up a deficiency in Greek, so I enrolled in a six-week intensive summer class. Our first assignment, due the next day: memorize and say the Greek alphabet in less than fifteen seconds and memorize over one hundred cognate vocabulary words. I was definitely in over my head. But that first day of class our professor taught a lesson that has had a far greater impact on me than the Greek alphabet. He drew a long line on the board, starting on the bottom left and rising steeply up to the right.

He then explained that this arrow represented the amount of

Figure 3.2. Knowledge accumulated

knowledge that we were going to accumulate during the next three years. Then he drew a second arrow, starting at the same place but with a much shallower incline, saying, "The second line represents the amount of knowledge that you will be able to put into practice." He added, "Beware of the gap." Those words have stuck with me.

Figure 3.3. Knowledge accumulated vs. knowledge practiced

Although I tried hard to "beware of the gap," I've often wondered whether I was better or worse off at the end of seminary. In one sense I knew more and could, therefore, live up to more, but in the other sense, I was now responsible for a lot of information that I had not yet experienced or put into practice. Perhaps the most important aspect of that lesson was that I no longer pursued knowledge as an end in itself. Knowledge was important, but something lay beyond knowledge: transformed behavior triggered by obedience. Even though my knowledge of God's Word would always be partial and my experience would always be incomplete, I could learn to hear and obey the voice of God. That could make a difference for the kingdom of God.

Clearly, obedience matters.

Jesus said, "Why do you call Me, 'Lord, Lord,' and *do not do what* I say? Everyone who comes to Me and hears My words *and acts on them* . . . is like a man building a house, who dug deep and laid a foundation on the rock" (Lk 6:46-48).

Or again, "That slave who knew his master's will and did not get ready *or act in accord* with his will, will receive many lashes" (Lk 12:47).

Jesus expected obedience to his word, not simply mental assent to accumulated knowledge.

In the first half of his letter to the Ephesians, Paul lays out the theological foundations of our spiritual identity as disciples in the body of Christ. Then, in the second half, he expresses his expectations of how disciples should behave as a result of this knowledge: tell the truth rather than lie, work rather than steal, forgive rather than brood, encourage rather than gossip, give thanks rather than indulge in raunchy humor.[7]

Paul unequivocally expects the Ephesian disciples to take action based on his teaching. "Therefore be careful *how you walk*, not as unwise men, but as wise, making the most of your time, because the days are evil. So then do not be foolish, but understand *what the will of the Lord is*" (Eph 5:15-17). We probably all know someone who has said, "The Lord told me to _____," without confirming through Scripture and the community of other believers whether that was, indeed, the Lord's voice. Perhaps we also know others who, after years of acquiring knowledge, know more than they practice.

Neither Jesus nor Paul expected uninformed obedience. Nor did they expect informed disobedience. They expected a reciprocal relationship between knowledge and experience formed by obedience. Every new truth requires some adjustment to our behavior, some essential step of obedience. And every step of obedience rests on the knowledge of Christ and his word.

The disciple package comes with assembly required. Growth as disciples of Jesus requires both knowledge *and* experience, connected by obedience. Obedience is the bridge between knowledge and experience that not only accomplishes the will of God in the world, but also brings about transformation at the deepest levels.

OBEDIENCE GOES TO THE HEART OF CULTURE

Paul Hiebert developed a model of culture that contains four concentric circles.[8] The outer, or fourth, circle represents social institutions such as politics, law, religion, economics, aesthetics, technology and social organization. When people travel to other countries and cultures, this level is what they see and experience. The third circle represents the cognitive level, including assumptions, thinking patterns held in common and the notion of what is true and false (T/F). The second circle depicts the affective level, common assumptions about emotions, beauty, style and the value of feelings. These can be summarized as likes and dislikes (L/D). Finally, at the core or center circle lies the evaluative level, that which people value most and may be willing to die for, that which is right and wrong (R/W). Worldview is represented by the inner three circles, forming the heart of culture.

A doctor who smokes cigarettes is an example of a person who has

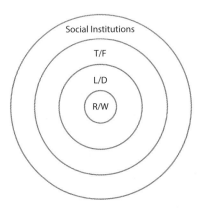

Figure 3.4. A model of culture. Based on figure 8 from Paul Hiebert, *Anthropological Insights for Missionaries* (Baker, 1985), p. 46.

access to all of the information regarding carcinogens and the delete-rious effects on the body of smoking (T/F), but the feeling produced by smoking (L/D) outweighs the knowledge (T/F) and determines his behavior. Or, in a positive example, a doctor who enters a zone with an active Ebola outbreak may do so because of a deep sense that it is right to do so (R/W), even though she may be afraid (L/D), knowing all of the risks (T/F). Life-changing decisions usually arise from the center and move outward.

The transmission of truth statements, or knowledge of the Bible, operates at the cognitive level of worldview. For those truth state-ments to penetrate through the affective level and bring change to the evaluative level, a person must engage with the truth through experi-ential obedience. Obedience is the key that brings about the gradual transformation of all three levels of worldview and accomplishes God's will at the same time. Baptism, for example, is a momentous event in many cultures, perhaps because it is the visible step of obe-dience that has the potential to move the cognitive understanding of faith and repentance into the evaluative core.

Ted Ward, noted educational theorist and teacher, introduced the concept of a split rail fence to represent balance between the two slider switches of knowledge and experience. The top rail corresponds to knowledge or theory, and the bottom rail is experience. The rails are connected by posts that represent opportunities to discuss how to integrate the two rails. He frequently said, "There is nothing as prac-tical as good theory."[9]

To be able to discuss the tension between knowledge and experience with people who represent different cultures provides a great advantage. Some may have come from a background where there is a high degree of healthy tension in this pair of slider switches. Others may have de-fault settings in one direction or the other. Postmodern cultures, for instance, are drowning in knowledge, but often without any sure guide to understand what information is important to put into practice.

Experience without knowledge. Those coming from a Muslim culture may have a highly developed commitment to certain behavioral experiences, but little knowledge. A good Muslim dutifully performs the five pillars of Islam: he or she prays five times a day, fasts during Ramadan, gives alms, recites the creed and goes on pilgrimage to Mecca at least once in a lifetime. Learning the Qur'an in an unknown language does not matter, because knowledge of the truth or of God's Word does not inform their experience. Certain behaviors become an end in themselves, without the transformative effect provided by dynamic obedience.

The advantage of this cultural disposition is that people may be quick to ask what obedience might be required when they discover new truth about God. One worker reported that the first time some former Muslim men read the verses that emphasized the importance of forgiving others their sins, they were astounded. In their culture restoring honor through vengeance was a deeply held value. One of the men said, "But Jesus said it, so it must be true, and therefore we must forgive." Willingness to obey drove them toward transformation of the values at the core of their worldview.

Knowledge without experience. On the opposite end of the spectrum is knowledge without any corresponding expectation of experience through obedience.

For a three-year period in the early '80s, I represented TEAM on the board of a seminary in Venezuela. The seminary had been founded by North American missionaries and was patterned after a well-known seminary in the United States. Robert, a board member representing another mission agency, and I were each working to start a new church in the general vicinity of the seminary, and we both hoped to partner with students. We discovered, however, that students worked enthusiastically with us during their first year of seminary, participated only sporadically the second year, and by the third year no longer even attended meetings of the church. When I spoke with the student who had been helping at our church, he responded that the academic work was his priority. He couldn't sacrifice the time necessary to participate in the church.

Since both Robert and I were on the board, we brought the matter up for discussion, inquiring about the practical work experience required at the school. We discovered that although students were required to work in a church on the weekends, that assignment did not affect their grades one way or the other. I questioned this policy, and the rector of the seminary quoted Isaiah, saying that his word will not return to him void, without accomplishing what he desires,[10] and that if they taught the Bible, everything else would take care of itself. Obedience was not required. Behavior was a hoped-for byproduct.

Knowledge and experience without obedience. Perhaps one of the most damaging distortions of these slider switches is that of the Pharisees. They observed rigid rules of behavior that came from a systematic understanding of the Mosaic law, but in doing so, they missed the dynamic process of obedience to God. They were so sure they were right in what they believed and practiced that God himself could not persuade them otherwise. Unfortunately, this kind of arrogance is common to many cultures, and, in particular to those with highly religious backgrounds. Tom Hovestol has written a very helpful book on this subject, *Extreme Righteousness: Seeing Ourselves in the Pharisees.*[11]

Knowledge and experience with obedience. Today there is much renewed interest in spiritual direction and spiritual guidance, helping new disciples increase their ability to hear and obey God. Ignatius, one of the early church fathers, taught much about hearing and obedience. He signed many of his letters with a short prayer, reflecting the deep desire of a disciple to hear and obey: "May it please the supreme and divine Goodness to give us all abundant grace ever to know his most holy will and perfectly to fulfill it."[12] Ignatius also recommended three simple prayers: "What have I done for Christ? What am I doing for Christ? What ought I to do for Christ?"

What would happen if, at the end of any church service, everyone were asked to listen in silence to the voice of God, with the following question in mind: "As a result of what I have seen and heard this morning, is there anything that Christ wants me to do?"

EXAMPLES OF HEARING AND OBEYING

Asking Jesus what he wants you to do. One day while Bakht Singh was still living with the Haywards, he received a call from someone asking him to speak about India and his newfound faith. He immediately accepted. Edith Hayward overheard the conversation. After Bakht Singh hung up the telephone, she questioned him. Had he inquired of the Lord? Bakht Singh argued that he was doing a good thing, so why shouldn't he make a decision on the spot? Later he was convicted that he had, indeed, agreed to accept the obligation on his own; he decided from then on he would do nothing without first asking the Lord. This principle was one of three that guided his work for the rest of his life. He was not ignorant of the Scripture, studying and preaching constantly. But he lived his life from then on in simple obedience to whatever the Lord told him. Edith Hayward, asking a simple question after overhearing one side of a telephone conversation, engaged Bakht Singh in a process of making disciples through obedience.

Doing what Jesus tells you. Rachel led children's ministry in her church in the city of Vienna. She effectively developed curricula, trained teachers and taught children. She felt fulfilled and satisfied with her ministry. After a period away from Vienna communicating with churches in America, Rachel and her husband, Dan, returned to a new apartment in Vienna. To drive to the multipurpose building where the church met, however, she either had to drive past several brothels or go around. Either way created a problem. Going past made her sad. Going around made her feel guilty. As Rachel drove to the ministry center, the Lord began to "tap her on the shoulder," saying,

"Rachel, I want you to do something about this." Rachel's first response was, "But Lord, I don't know anything about it." Or, "Ask someone else." But the Lord kept prodding.

Finally Rachel decided to act. She wrote an email to several other people in Vienna from other churches, inviting them to join her for prayer one evening about the issue. To her amazement, twenty-three people from nine churches joined her that night. They too had been hearing the voice of the Holy Spirit talking to them about the very same problem. As they prayed and searched the Scriptures together, they were convinced that God had spoken, and they decided to obey.

Prostitution is legal in Austria, but many women are caught in the net of human trafficking. Slick promoters in Africa or Romania promise a young woman a job in a restaurant or as a nanny and, upon arrival, they remove her passport, requiring up to 60,000 Euros for its return. Then they sign her up with the labor department as a prostitute, effectively trapping her in that profession.

Rachel and twenty-three other people, in obedience to the command of Jesus, started something that has since demonstrated the love of Christ to many women on the streets of Vienna. Some have been rescued, others have been saved from getting involved to begin with, and the organization they founded now has a seat on the "EU Civil Platform Against Trafficking in Human Beings" and has spoken at several UN functions.

Never underestimate the explosive potential of a single act of obedience.

Trusting and obeying, despite possible persecution. Salim, a Muslim raised in Indonesia, hated Christians, persecuting them whenever he could. He became ill, but no doctors seemed to be able to help him. He grew worse and worse, eventually fearing for his life. One day he was passing by the home of a Christian who called out to him.

The Christian said, "I know that you are sick. I can't do anything to help, but I know someone who heals. Would you like me to pray to

Jesus for you?" Salim responded, "All right, I'll come to your house so that you can pray for me. If Jesus heals me, I will follow him. If he doesn't, I'll kill you."

The Christian in humble obedience prayed for Salim, trusting that God had told him to do so. Salim said that he felt something like an electric shock pulsating from his head downward, out to his fingertips and eventually to his toes. In that moment he was completely healed, and became a follower of Jesus Christ.

Later Salim formed an organization which began schools for transmigrant Muslims moving from Java, and then helped TEAM missionaries begin a community center as part of that organization. The simple act of obedience of a humble Christian not only changed Salim's life, it changed the entire landscape for hundreds of Muslim youth.

Staying accountable to the body. The organization 3DM[13] promotes the principle of low control and high accountability. In the leadership development groups called huddles, participants are regularly asked the question, "What has the Lord said to you recently?" They expect the Lord to set the agenda, not the leader. After someone answers the question, the group confirms whether or not this was the Lord's voice, informed by the Word of God. After the group confirms that what a person thinks he or she has heard is from the Lord, the leaders asks, "What are you going to do to implement and obey what you have heard?" The group again reflects on the answer, confirms once again, then builds in accountability: "How will you hold yourself accountable to do what we have talked about?" They integrate the collective wisdom of the group, the Word of God and obedience, leading to transformation.

Embracing the messiness. Learning to hear and obey is a minute-by-minute, daily affair that rarely fits into a nice neat program.

Yelitza, a twenty-something, classy single woman, arrived at our meeting in high heels and tight jeans, having just stubbed out a cigarette from her third pack that day. She was hanging on to the arm of her boyfriend, Manuel, who had invited her to this new church where he knew some "gringos" who spoke English. She had no idea that she was arriving at a course for new disciples, but she was interested in practicing her English.

Our first church in Maracay, Venezuela, had several people who had made a decision to follow the Lord but had not yet been baptized. We did what seemed like the best next step in starting our church: we designed a pre-planned, nicely packaged, theologically correct series of ten Bible studies, covering the basics of the Christian life. Manuel said he had made a decision to follow the Lord, so we invited him to come. When Yelitza showed up with him for the third class, we were surprised, but decided to continue the series even though she had made no previous decision to follow Jesus.

One of the last classes was on baptism, and we were thrilled when several indicated they wanted to be baptized. When Yelitza said she wanted to be baptized, we had to stop and ask if she had ever accepted Jesus as her Lord. She had missed the first class that covered that important step of obedience. We shared the need for her to talk to the Lord, confess her sins and invite Jesus into her life, giving her a simple tract explaining the basic steps to faith in Jesus.

As she made her way by bus to her mother's home that weekend, she began reading the Bible, going over some of the passages we had studied together. As she read the Scripture, ash from her cigarette fell onto the pages of the Bible. She attempted to brush off the ash, leaving an ugly black smear on the page. Suddenly she was overcome with a sense of shame, and immediately reached for the simple tract we had given her. As she read through the tract, she felt God's call on her life and gave her life to Jesus. The next day, when she reached for her first cigarette, she felt sick and decided to try later. Three times that day she tried to smoke but felt nauseated. Finally, she decided that she didn't really like smoking anyway, and never touched a cigarette again. Her crash course in obedience to the Holy Spirit had begun. We didn't even know that she was addicted to cigarettes, and we had not included material on conquering addictions in the course we taught.

Yelitza was baptized along with several others a few weeks later. After she had made the decision to follow Jesus, she realized very quickly that she was going to have to change her lifestyle. Somehow she knew that her behavior had to change. Because her father had died while in the Venezuelan navy, she had been living on a government pension and would often spend her nights in discotheques and her days on the beach. Now she wanted to work and go back to school, but she needed a place to live while she got her papers in order and searched for a job. She shared her dilemma with us, and we decided to invite her to live with us for a few weeks. Little did we realize that the weeks would turn into months, and the months would turn into more than two years. Yelitza became a member of our family, earning our love and respect as a younger sister.

As the days went by, Yelitza would come to the table with questions tumbling out: Why did the Bible say this? What did it mean when the Bible said that? What should she do about the various situations of her life? How should she respond to her cousins who were ridiculing her? How should she share her faith with her brother? If her new boss wanted her to cheat on something, what should she say? Yelitza's sister had died in an automobile accident earlier; should she adopt her sister's daughter? We began to see life through her eyes and would share what we could, often praying with her. She began to integrate biblical truth into her life. More than once I would have to look for Gleason Archer's *Encyclopedia of Bible Difficulties* in order to find answers to her questions. Years later, she began serving as a missionary to a small town in western Venezuela, where she started a church through children's ministry, then ministry to the mothers, and finally to whole families.

As I look back on Yelitza's story, I am intrigued by the contrast between the slider switch settings of the discipleship course we planned and executed, and the messy, human, unplanned and unpredictable disciple making that happened when Yelitza lived with us.

DISCIPLES LEARN TO HEAR AND OBEY

At the end of his life, Jesus could say to his disciples, "The world may learn that I love the Father and do exactly what my Father has commanded me" (Jn 14:31 NIV). Then, speaking directly to the Father, "I have brought you glory by completing the work you gave me to do" (Jn 17:4 NIV). Imagine what would happen if every disciple of Jesus Christ would follow his example and be able to say, "I do exactly what Jesus commands me."

Jesus is in charge. He is leading. Learning to listen and obey, a fundamental principle of discipleship, honors him, fulfills his will and extends his kingdom. As we join one another in this journey of obedience, we grow closer to him and to one another.

Disciples Develop
Relational Interdependence

Individualism and Collectivism

There is one body.

EPHESIANS 4:4 NIV

Our team was tired. We had wrestled with a strategic organizational issue for most of the day. No matter which way we looked at the issue, obstacles abounded. Everyone had participated, but it seemed hopeless. Toward the end of the day, we stopped to pray. For the next forty-five minutes, we poured out our thoughts and hearts to the Lord, admitting that we were stuck and asking for help. Then, exhausted, we adjourned the meeting until the next day.

The next morning, one team member said overnight he had a thought that might resolve the issue. He proceeded to explain. As he sketched out his ideas on the board, all the various pieces began to come together. A potential solution appeared. With the Lord's direction, together we unlocked a thorny issue that had been troubling the organization for decades.

No one individual had been able to find the solution, although each had contributed. As a community, calling on the Lord together, we succeeded. We demonstrated the truth of the proverb, "None of us is as smart as all of us,"[1] adding, "particularly when the Lord is leading." Over the next ten years, the validity of that solution became increasingly apparent.

Our experience highlights another principle of disciple making: disciples develop relational interdependence.

God loves individuals deeply—he knows and values each one. He knows each by name. No community of disciples would be possible without committed, growing individuals who have a personal relationship with Jesus. When the slider switch corresponding to the individual is set too high, however, and that corresponding to community is set too low, building relationships can be elusive, friendships remain shallow, teamwork is challenging and partnerships are difficult. Fragmentation and alienation are too often the result.

God loves the community of Christ. He rejoices in the love, unity and harmony when each individual functions as part of the whole. But when the slider switch corresponding to community is set all the way to the top and that corresponding to the individual is set all the way to the bottom, equally destructive results can take place. Visitors may feel like outsiders after years of attending the same group, individuals may lose their own sense of value and contribution, and decision making may become gridlocked.

When disciples develop relational interdependence, real community flourishes, teamwork emerges, mutual trust and commitment build. We develop a collective vision both for the church and for mission, within which each individual has a specific and meaningful role. *My* individual work has value, because it contributes to *our* collective work.

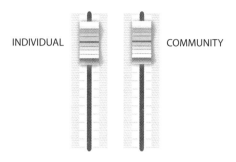

INDIVIDUAL   COMMUNITY

Figure 4.1. Individual and community

MAINTAINING BIBLICAL TENSION:
INDIVIDUAL AND COMMUNITY

The Trinity beautifully demonstrates relational interdependence, where individual and community are held in perfect tension. Each member of the Trinity is a whole person with individual responsibilities, but they function as a collective unity to such a degree that they are one God.

Jesus says, "All authority in heaven and on earth has been given to me. Therefore go and make disciples of all nations, baptizing them in the name of the Father and of the Son and of the Holy Spirit, and teaching them to obey everything I have commanded you" (Mt 28:18-20 NIV).

Jesus is the only one who can truly call himself the center of the universe,[2] because the Trinity has given him "all authority in heaven and on earth." From that position of singular authority, he commands that we all give our allegiance back to the Trinity.

Just as Jesus is complete within the collective of the Trinity, so too I am complete within the community of Christ. The promise of Jesus' presence is not mine alone; it is mine as shared with all those who bow the knee and proclaim Jesus as Lord.[3]

Larry Crabb, a licensed psychotherapist, describes the delight that the

Trinity has in working together: "Imagine the sheer delight of enjoying perfect relationships with two others with no fear of things turning sour, a community of three cut from the same fabric yet unmistakably distinct. . . . Their purpose in creating people was to invite us to the party."[4]

Jesus introduces each new believer to the community of the Godhead and to the community of the body of Christ. The individual self becomes whole as each one's unique gifts and contribution are fully realized. A party indeed!

Ruth Haley Barton, reflecting on her work in spiritual formation ministry to pastors and Christian leaders, extends this same point: "The root meaning of *community* is to 'come together' in 'unity.'. . . We are unified by our commitment to be transformed in Christ's presence through the work of the Holy Spirit so we can discern and do the will of God as we are guided by the Spirit."[5]

Both of these counselors have worked with numerous people who are caught up in the blistering pace of ministry in an individualist context. They are convinced that the solution is to reintroduce individual people to the delights and depths of true community, to find collective identity in Christ. Crabb and Barton are reintroducing healthy tension between identity as an individual and as a community, based on a deep understanding of the Trinity and the Word of God.

These two slider switches reveal an astonishing oversight: most translators of the Bible into English overlook the difference between the plural form of the pronoun *you* and the singular form of *you*. Consider the following passage from Ephesians:

> For this reason I too, having heard of the faith in the Lord Jesus which exists among you and your love for all the saints, do not cease giving thanks for you, while making mention of you in my prayers; that the God of our Lord Jesus Christ, the Father of glory, may give to you a spirit of wisdom and of revelation in the knowledge of Him. (Eph 1:15-17)

Every use of the word "you" is in plural form. Here is how it should read:

> For this reason I too, having heard of the faith in the Lord Jesus which exists among you [all] and your [plural] love for all the saints, do not cease giving thanks for you [all], while making mention of you [all] in my prayers; that the God of our Lord Jesus Christ, the Father of glory, may give to you [all] a spirit of wisdom and of revelation in the knowledge of Him. (Eph 1:15-17)

Every time Paul writes the word *you* in Ephesians he means the whole group, the entire body of Christ in Ephesus. Reading the Bible with the plural inserted, as happens in other languages, transforms our understanding. Instead of thinking *me* every time I see the word *you*, I learn to think *us*—the body of Christ.

Consider how the quote from Matthew 28:18-20 changes in meaning:

> All authority in heaven and on earth has been given to me. Therefore go [plural] and make [plural] disciples of all nations, baptizing them in the name of the Father and of the Son and of the Holy Spirit, and teaching them to obey everything I have commanded you [all]. And surely I am with you [all] always, to the very end of the age. (NIV)

I've only demonstrated two short passages, but most English readers will be astounded at how often the word *you* occurs in the plural form, rather than the singular.

Beginning with a profound understanding of the collective nature of the body of Christ, however, sharpens the contrast when any passage focuses on the individual, as Paul does in the following statement:

> There is one body and one Spirit, just as also you [all] were called in one hope of your [plural] calling; one Lord, one faith, one baptism, one God and Father of all who is over all and through

all and in all. But *to each one of us* grace was given according to the measure of Christ's gift. (Eph 4:4-7)

God has the capacity to build one body out of millions of diverse individuals. Under his headship, that body has the capacity to accomplish infinitely more than any individual, even though he knows each individual personally, having given each one the gifts that he knows will best contribute to the whole.

CULTURAL MASTER SWITCHES: INDIVIDUALISM AND COLLECTIVISM

Any team of people who desire to do ministry together would do well to carefully and prayerfully evaluate their default settings with the continuum between the individual and community. Doing so will not happen quickly or easily. This set alone will cause teams to implode if they are unable to find settings on which they all agree. Let God lead a deep evaluation of these assumptions, adjusting methods to find those that will best build the body of Christ in each cultural context.

The way in which individuals relate to community has been widely studied by sociologists. Geert Hofstede carried out one of the first studies, published in 1980, compiling approximately 116,000 questionnaires from subsidiaries of a multinational business organization in forty nations.[6] Hofstede developed a scale of 0-100, with 100 being the most individually oriented and one being the most community oriented.

The three countries with the highest degree of individualism were the United States (91), Australia (90) and Great Britain (89). The three least individualist countries were Pakistan (14), Colombia (13) and Venezuela (12). My wife and I, with a cultural heritage from the United States, the most individually oriented country in the world, were living in Venezuela, the most community oriented in the world. No wonder we were confused.

Later, while working on my doctoral dissertation, I found answers to much of this confusion while doing my field research on the theme of collective identity and a counter theme of individual identity, generating insights that were of great help to us.[7]

In 1984, Michael Kearney identified seven worldview universals.[8] Three of the seven universals are the notions of self, other and relationship. Every culture of the world provides its people with assumptions defining the self, who others are and the relationships between them.

Elevating the individual. In a culture that elevates the individual, the self is an autonomous unit, capable of operating independently of others. Maturity is equated with self-sufficiency, self-reliance and autonomy. The self is a whole part, and value is derived by what each individual can do—his or her work. Others are viewed in precisely the same way—autonomous units, also capable of operating independently of others.

The relationship between self and others is generally defined by shallow ties, high mobility and a like-it-or-leave-it mentality. Many times the first question one asks in order to get to know others is, "What do you do?" Competition becomes a means of finding what one individual is good at doing, providing identity: a banker, teacher, lawyer, bricklayer and so on. Individuals view dependence on others with dread.

Individualism has a bright side and a dark side. Entrepreneurs, innovators, pioneers and explorers thrive on the bright side of individualism. No one would have ventured beyond the Mississippi into the Wild West of the United States if it had not been for some tough men and women who could face the winters alone, drag their wagons across mountains and wrest a living from the soil. Individuals take responsibility and are expected to accept the blame when something goes wrong.

On the dark side, however, selfishness, shallow relationships, alienation and narcissism wreak havoc with the soul. Individualist societies love to pin the blame on someone, preferably an individual. If a company does not perform according to expectations, the board fires the CEO who accepts responsibility and walks away.

Dark manifestations of individualism erode the social fabric. Narcissism, for instance, is on the rise in the United States: "We are in the midst of a 'narcissism epidemic,' concluded psychologists Jean M. Twenge and W. Keith Campbell in their book published in 2009. One study they describe showed that among a group of 37,000 college students, narcissistic personality traits rose just as quickly as obesity from the 1980s to the present."[9]

Individualism, taken to the extreme, ends in loss of meaning. The unnerving direction of individualism in the United States has been well documented. In 1985, a team of sociologists conducted extensive research on patterns of individualism in American life, recorded in the extremely thought-provoking book *Habits of the Heart*.

> We found all the classic polarities of American individualism still operating: the deep desire for autonomy and self-reliance combined with an equally deep conviction that life has no meaning unless shared with others in the context of community. . . . We are hesitant to articulate our sense that we need one another as much as we need to stand alone, for fear that if we did we would lose our independence altogether.[10]

With such pervasive default settings in individualist culture at large, we should not be surprised to find them influencing ideas of church and mission as much as they do.

In the church in the United States, individualism is thriving. Salvation is conferred on individuals. Individuals decide to come or go as they please, holding commitments quite loosely. Individuals make personal choices based on individual preferences, shopping for churches as they do for food or clothes.

Worship songs embrace the culture of individualism and are regularly punctuated with references to "me," "my" and "I." In one experiment, I counted the number of times that these pronouns occurred in two popular worship choruses. In two songs, "I" sang about "me" eighty-five times. The most egregious example is the song "Above All" that contains the phrase, "trampled on the ground, he took the fall, and thought of me, above all." In this song, we are led to believe that the Son of God, hanging on the cross, enduring unspeakable physical pain and spiritual separation from his eternal Father, thought of me, above all. Not you, or you, or you, but ME! This is errant nonsense—theological narcissism.

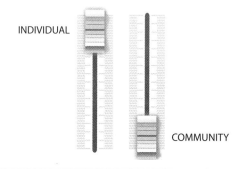

INDIVIDUAL

COMMUNITY

Figure 4.2. Individual high, community low

Individualism may be even more pervasive among missionaries from highly individualist cultures. Each individual missionary is expected to have received a call to mission, persuading others to embrace his or her individual call and to support it. Similarly, mission agencies evaluate individuals, process individuals, set up separate accounts for individuals and track the life cycles of individuals. Historically, individuals have made their way to a distant area of the world, often with very little guidance or collective wisdom concerning their personal ministry.

Elevating the community. In a culture that elevates community, the self is part of a whole, rather than a whole part. Maturity is carrying out one's role in the community to which one belongs. Interdependence is considered normal and everyone participates in decision making. Identity derives primarily from one's role as father, mother, brother, sister, son, daughter or neighbor. In contrast to competition, belonging is the greater value. Collective cultures place a high value on the honor of the community and avoiding shame. Isolation is viewed with dread.

Collectivism also has a bright side and a dark side.

On the bright side, people find a sense of belonging, they easily share what they have and their identity is rooted within sets of enduring relationships. Anthropologists refer to a phenomenon in collective societies known as "in group" and "out group" thinking. If you are "in" the group, you are really "in." In a collective society such as Venezuela, if you are part of the "in" group, the expression *mi casa es su casa* (my house is your house) truly applies.

On the dark side, however, collective pride can easily breed classism, apartheid, racism or tribalism, descending sometimes to genocide, as it did in Rwanda. If you are not "in" the group, you do not exist as a person and can easily be ignored or mistreated. Decision making can be extremely slow. Unbridled collectivism has proven particularly destructive in various parts of Africa whenever tribal prejudice has erupted, but the same tendencies appear in cliques, gangs or class groupings elsewhere.

Two aspects of a collective culture that affect ideas of church and mission are collective decision making, and shame and honor.

Because our office in Caracas was in a high-rise building, we were invited to the condominium association meetings. As soon as an item was introduced for a decision, everyone began speaking at once. If there were fifteen people in the room, at least fifteen conversations ensued. To someone from an individualist background, it appeared chaotic. Actually, everyone was listening to what all the others were saying. Any given individual did not know what he or she thought on the issue at hand until hearing what the others thought, particularly those whom they respected the most. After a period of time, the whole group was able to make a decision. If someone had tried to impose

Robert's Rules of Order, it would have destroyed the capacity of the group to make a good decision. Equally, forcing someone to take a position on the issue without understanding the thoughts of the rest of the group was a path to shame.

Since belonging to the group is of such high value, to be shamed or ridiculed brings dishonor to oneself and the whole group. In Venezuela, the expression for shame is *me da pena* ("it gives me shame"), and if someone has that feeling, nothing will move him or her.

Conflict resolution in collective societies often requires an intermediary who does not feel the shame. Gradually the mediator can bring the parties back together. The estranged parties know that the conflict is over when they can belong to the same group once more, participating in normal activities, without shame. Face-to-face encounters, where each is expected to shoulder his or her share of the blame or guilt, simply will not work.

Concepts of time. Cultural notions of time, another of Kearney's worldview universals, often coincide with and reinforce the worldview of the self and others.

I found how they related very soon after beginning our work. Our first church in Maracay was growing to the point that I could start visiting people during the week. A seminal book on pastoral methods I had read in seminary asserted that pastoral visitation was key to successful church growth. The well-known author calculated that a pastor should make four half-hour visits per afternoon. That number, multiplied by five afternoons, would yield twenty visits per week. He reasoned that in fifty weeks (two weeks for vacation), a good pastor could make one thousand per year. I set out for my first half-hour visit. I was in for a surprise.

Veronica was thrilled to receive me. Dropping in was perfectly acceptable. Cell phones had not yet come along, and applications for landlines had a seven-year waiting list, so neither Veronica nor we had phones in our homes. Veronica had three children, two still living at home in their fourth-floor apartment. All but the older brother were beginning to attend our church services. We began chatting about family, the neighborhood, the church. After about forty-five minutes, I glanced at my watch and realized that if I was going to achieve my goal of making four calls that afternoon, it was time to leave.

When I got up and mentioned that I would have to leave, Veronica looked at me with a startled expression and said, "What? Is this a medical visit?"[11] Chagrined, I sat down, apologizing for my unseemly haste. A little later she served small cups of strong sweet coffee, and we continued to chat. After approximately three hours of conversation—discussion about the Bible, the husband who had left her, concerns for her older son—and prayer together, it seemed appropriate to begin the process of saying goodbye. We stood up, chatted some more, moved to the front door, chatted on the balcony, and eventually I walked to the stairway, waving as I left.

My plan for one thousand visits a year was in shambles. However, almost thirty-five years later, we are still in touch with her family.

Real relationships endure over time. Efficient ones rarely do.

Without realizing it, I had made my measure of success a certain number of visits, rather than the relational connections that could be achieved. Real relationships and interdependence can rarely be contained or developed in half-hour linear time bites, and in a collective society like Venezuela, attempting it is counterproductive. In a collective culture, time is always the servant of relationships, not the other way around.

I did not yet understand that I was living in one of the most collectively oriented cultures in the world.[12] In my individualist culture, relationships fit in the pre-designed box of a personal time schedule; in Veronica's collective culture, the box of time expanded to fit the relationship. In her view, being with people always superseded linear time and its corollary—efficiency. I learned later that about three hours was normal for a good visit. Anything shorter was close to an insult—like treating people as cogs in a machine. The seminary course did not reach across cultures. I thought about writing to the professor, saying that his methods would not work in Venezuela, but I never did.

Individualism and collectivism have to be held in tension for the body of Christ to function properly. In order to grow, disciples must develop relational interdependence.

EXAMPLES OF MERGING AND BALANCING INDIVIDUAL WITH COMMUNITY

Gathering in households. After I had begun to understand the importance of collective thinking, I received an invitation to study the Bible with Evelyn and her teenage children. I did not want to divide the household, so I said to Evelyn, "If you and I study the Bible together with your children, and if you decide to make some fundamental changes in what you think and how you act, it could bring serious division into your marriage. That is the last thing I want to do. Talk to your husband, and if he agrees to join us, then we will have the Bible study."

Three times the husband agreed to come at the appointed time. Three times he did not arrive. Each time I left without having the Bible study. The fourth time, as I was leaving I saw him drive into the parking area in front of their apartment building. I greeted him, and shared something from the Bible study with him in the parking lot. Later he told me that he had tried to avoid me again, but had mistimed his arrival. From that time on, he joined us and I worked with the entire household. Today both Evelyn and Alex are using their gifts in service to the Lord.

In Afghanistan, the household is the primary meeting place of the body of Christ. Believers gather in cells of two or three, meeting in restaurants and teashops, and they gather with their households. They do not have the option of large Sunday morning meetings; each leader of the household is responsible for the spiritual development of his or her extended family. A missionary hearing this explained suggested, "Maybe the cell and the household are the essential gathering places for the body of Christ. If believers have the option of gathering in larger groups, such as missional communities or 'crowd' gatherings on Sunday morning, that is a bonus. But if all you have is the 'crowd' gathering on Sunday, and don't have cells and households, you probably have to think some more about what you are doing."

Working in teams. Working on an interdependent team is not necessarily easier, but it is better. As the illustration at the beginning of the chapter suggests, not only can teams of disciples develop all of the potential described by Katzenbach in *Wisdom of Teams*,[13] but they have the spiritual power of the presence of Christ in their midst. Teams have a unique capacity to demonstrate the body of Christ in all of its beauty and power, which a group of loosely collected individuals does not have.

Teams gather around the presence of Christ to discern his will and carry it out. The will of God, discerned and confirmed by the Word of God and by the members of the team, becomes the galvanizing vision for which each individual contribution is essential.

Love and unity on a team, or "oneness," can always be threatened by disagreement and disunity, but each time disciples forgive one another and work through these issues, love and unity become stronger, and the team grows more spiritually powerful. I learned, after years of working on teams, to welcome conflict as an opportunity to grow deeper in love and unity.

Creating islands of timelessness. Relational interdependence cannot develop in neatly arranged half-hour segments. When inviting others into our lives, giving a start time is helpful, but leaving the end time open-ended allows for relational interdependence to begin to grow. Perhaps the best way to think of this is a family reunion or vacation, in which interactions and activities occur spontaneously and last as long as necessary, without someone limiting everything by the clock.

Greeting one another. In a collective society such as Venezuela, the way people greet one another and the way they say goodbye provides a constant barometer of the warmth of the relationship. If someone enters a room and does not greet all the people, the ones who do not receive a greeting will immediately begin to wonder what is wrong with the relationship. A cold or short greeting, without an accompanying touch, is also a sign that something is not right. If people leave without saying goodbye, without a word, a kiss on the cheek or a touch on the shoulder, then the overwhelming impression is that something has gone wrong. Those who were ignored will do everything possible in the ensuing days to find out and rectify whatever problem might exist. Conversely, if the greetings are warm and effusive, expressed to each individual present, then the group knows that all is well.

Those from an individualist background may feel awkward greeting one another and saying goodbye to one another when joining or leaving a group, but doing so is a healthy way of affirming relational interdependence.

Pledging friendship to one another. One Sunday in Venezuela, it was Angel's turn to preach. The chosen passage was the story of David and Jonathan pledging undying friendship to each other and greeting one another expressively (and appropriately in their culture). "David got up from the south side of the stone and bowed down before Jonathan three times, with his face to the ground. Then they kissed each other and wept together" (1 Sam 20:41 NIV).

We had discussed the passage together the previous Wednesday, and the part that I had seen, from my Western perspective, was how the mantle of leadership was passing from Jonathan to David. As Angel studied the passage, however, the part that he saw was the moment that two friends decided together that their friendship would endure as long as they were alive, expressed in the greeting and in the oath that they took with one another. "Go in peace, for we have sworn friendship with each other in the name of the Lord, saying, 'The LORD is witness between you and me, and between your descendants and my descendants forever'" (1 Sam 20:42 NIV). I was amazed that I had missed something so apparent in the passage.

The Holy Spirit spoke to my soul through Angel that morning. How often do friends pledge friendship with one another in an individualist society? Normally, the only acceptable place for such a thing is marriage vows, and even those are often conditional upon premarital agreements. But two friends? It does not happen very often. For those from an individualist background, such commitments impede independence.

Several years later, a couple we had grown to know and love had to move to another location. They came to Kris and me saying, "This relationship is important to us. We want it to continue. Can we continue to meet, even if we move farther away?" With Angel's lesson in mind, we agreed, and the relationship has endured. All of us have been enriched and blessed by the commitment we made that day.

Remembering where we all belong. Jesus is on a mission to redeem the lost and to reconcile all things to himself, to save the planet and to complete the greatest creation of all time—the body of Christ. He is finding the lost and broken, making them whole. He is looking for people from every tribe, people, language and nation to assemble around the throne. He is setting up his kingdom, a kingdom in which all those who become his disciples will rule as a kingdom of priests and a holy nation.[14]

If I learn to follow Jesus and obey him, I join others on their journey as disciples, and we make disciples of each other. As more and more people join our pilgrimage, we grow closer together and move closer to the same grand event—the wedding feast of the Lamb. I am not submerged by a growing number of pilgrims; rather, my soul is enlarged as it connects with all of the others. We all grow closer to Jesus.

Some good friends once invited Kris and me to attend a football game at the University of Michigan. Here's how it felt: We leave our home early on a Saturday morning to arrive on time. We drive for five hours in order to have lunch with our friends before the game. When we start out, I cannot tell if anyone else on the road has the same destination. As we cross the state line into Michigan, however, I begin to notice others joining the procession. Flags, colors and mascots begin appearing in car windows. We pass a large RV, completely painted in blue and gold. At the exit to the stadium we are bumper to bumper with everyone else. By the time we walk across the final street to the stadium, we are part of a great multitude, all united in a common vision to win that football game. It would be impossible to get to the game without joining the streaming crowd.

Joining this multitude on game day is but a tiny example of the growing church of Jesus Christ. Millions of disciples across the globe are all traveling to the throne room, in eager anticipation of the greatest day in the history of the world—the day when the body of Christ will be fully complete and we will come face-to-face with our Lord and Master. What a journey to be on together!

DISCIPLES DEVELOP RELATIONAL INTERDEPENDENCE

Relational interdependence affirms the value of the community and the value of the individual. Each individual is affirmed within the whole community, and the potential of the community is increased by the contribution of each individual. Whether someone is a part of a collective culture or a culture that elevates the individual, the community can accomplish more than anyone can alone. Disciples develop relational interdependence. Together is better.

However, relationships developed just for the sake of relationship will usually turn sour. At this point, other principles of disciple making come into play. We must let God lead, and we need one another to discern his leading and to carry it out in obedience. Learning to do mission together will in turn lead to relational interdependence. When that relational interdependence is characterized by love and unity, then the world notices. Jesus prays "that all of them may be one, Father, just as you are in me and I am in you. May they also be in us so that the world may believe that you have sent me" (Jn 17:21 NIV). Letting God lead, hearing and obeying together, will create a channel for his love to the world.

Disciples Do
What Love Requires

Gospel Truth and Works Justice

*If I speak in the tongues of men or of angels, but
do not have love, I am only a resounding
gong or a clanging symbol.*

I CORINTHIANS 13:1 NIV

Returning to our home one day in Venezuela, I noticed a truck parked in front of our house with someone working under the hood. After pulling in, I walked up and asked what was wrong. He responded that the battery had died. I sympathized, because batteries in the tropical climate often seemed to last just a little longer than the six-month warranty. I offered to give him a jump, which he accepted gratefully. Once the truck started, we chatted for a few minutes. He had noticed the sign above our garage with the words *Congregación Bíblica*. I explained a little of what we were doing, and then he drove off.

A few weeks later, a mother and her young daughter knocked on our door. They were in trouble. Her husband had left her, she had no income and food was running out. We quickly offered to help with some food and supplies, but she refused. She wanted to study the Bible with us; she needed hope much more than she needed food. So we gathered around a table, showing her how to understand the contents of the Bible, reading and discussing some key passages and praying with her. I'm sure that we gave her some supplies as well, but what she really wanted was food for her soul.

As I reflected on these two incidents, I realized that in the case of the driver, it would have been foolish to insist on communicating the gospel before I helped start his truck. But with the lady and her daughter, to insist on helping her physical needs before sharing hope in Jesus would have been equally foolish.

In both cases, the fundamental principle was to do what love required. This principle spans any cultural context, seamlessly combining word and works, truth and justice.

The 1989 Lausanne congress in Manila recognized the tension between word and works, truth and justice, affirming this principle: "As we proclaim the love of God we must be involved in loving service, as we preach the Kingdom of God we must be committed to its demands of justice and peace.... We also affirm that good news and good works are inseparable."[1]

Love extends to the whole person: body, mind and soul.

This principle may elicit a "Well, duh!" response. Of course we should love our neighbor as ourselves. Like the other disciple-making principles, however, culture creates powerful filters that easily distort how we carry it out.

LOVING OUR NEIGHBOR CONNECTS WORD AND WORKS, TRUTH AND JUSTICE

For the first few decades of my adult life, I believed in a definition of the gospel that consisted minimally of four propositions: First, God loves us. Second, all humans have sinned against God and are separated from him. Third, Jesus has paid the price for that sin through his death and atonement. Fourth, we can have eternal life if we will accept the sacrifice that he has made and repent of our sin. I had been taught that these propositions represented the "word," the "truth" or the "gospel." My responsibility as a disciple was to do evangelism, which I understood to mean that I had to convince as many people as possible of the validity of these four propositions.

I heard many sermons which emphasized how important it was to share these propositions with others, doing evangelism, and took well-designed classes in seminary on how to create opportunities to share these propositions with others.

I do not remember taking one single course or seminar on how to love my neighbor.

As time went on, I heard the stories of a wide variety of people who came to Jesus. I was increasingly impressed with the unique way God worked with each individual. Why did no two people come to Jesus the same way, if the same four propositions were essential for everyone to know? Even more confounding, if these propositions were the gospel, how was it possible for Jesus to preach the gospel when he had not yet died?

I began to worry that defining the gospel as simply the four propositions had more to do with a desire to mass-produce Christians than it did with biblical truth. What had been lost in the process of creating the simple, transferable and memorable guide to sharing the gospel that I had learned?

What if the gospel is Jesus himself, in all his power, mystery and glory? What if the gospel is the transformative encounter between Jesus and any living person who seeks him? What if the gospel is Jesus loving you and me, and loving others through us? What if the gospel is contained in the command, "Love your neighbor as yourself"? That is what Jesus did when he was incarnated into this world.

Combined, the four rational propositions represent one of the slider switches, often referred to as the "word" or "truth." The other slider switch is the demonstration of those truths through the lives of Jesus' disciples as they get involved with others, often referred to as "works" or "justice."

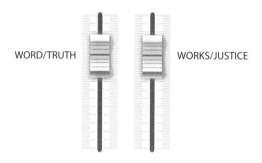

WORD/TRUTH   WORKS/JUSTICE

Figure 5.1. Word/truth and works/justice

When the slider switch corresponding to "word" is set high, propositional truth about Jesus predominates. When the slider switch corresponding to "works" is set high, actions predominate.

The principle of loving our neighbor, however, forces both switches into dynamic tension with one another. In order to love our neighbor, we have to know our neighbors well enough to know what love requires.

MAINTAINING BIBLICAL TENSION: WORD AND WORKS, TRUTH AND JUSTICE

Jesus preached the gospel of the kingdom. The currency of that kingdom is love. "Love one another, just as I have loved you" (Jn 15:12). "Love your neighbor as yourself" (Mt 22:39). "Love your enemies" (Lk 6:27). "If we love one another, God abides in us, and His love is perfected in us" (1 Jn 4:12).

The command to love our neighbor is repeated often, but nowhere does Scripture tell us that our principal duty is to evangelize our neighbor. Loving our neighbor may certainly include sharing those four propositions, but it may just as likely be a multitude of other actions that would be a legitimate response of love. Love desires the deepest good for the whole person.

Loving our neighbor—customized, not mass-produced. Loving our neighbor takes thousands of forms. No two stories of how someone comes to Jesus are the same; each is unique. To the Samaritan woman, Jesus was the living water.[2] To the Jews at Pentecost, Jesus was the one whom they had crucified and before whom they needed to repent.[3] To the jailer of Philippi, Jesus was the one who could give joy to God's servants when they were harshly treated and whose gracious response to him preserved the jailer's own life.[4] To the well-heeled young nobleman, Jesus was the one who could see what was blocking his path to eternal life. Jesus looked at him and loved him. He did not see him as an object or number; he saw him as a complete person.[5] To the Roman military officer, he was the one who healed his servant.[6] To the Ethiopian diplomat, he was the one who fulfilled the prophecies of Isaiah.[7] To the two on the road to Emmaus, Jesus was the one who broke bread with them.[8] Good news? Jesus—living, healing, sympathizing, teaching, saving, ruling and reigning as King.[9]

When we come face-to-face with Jesus himself (not just truths about him), life is turned upside down. Word and works go hand in hand. Truth and justice greet each other. Jesus is present.

Loving our neighbor—the whole person. The book of James is written with this set of slider switches clearly in mind.

> What good is it, my brothers and sisters, if someone claims to have faith but has no deeds? Can such faith save them? Suppose a brother or a sister is without clothes and daily food. If one of you says to them, "Go in peace; keep warm and well fed," but does nothing about their physical needs, what good is it? In the same way, faith by itself, if it is not accompanied by action, is dead. (Jas 2:14-17 NIV)

In the case of a mission hospital, love will not be satisfied with healing the body and not the soul. Nor will love be satisfied with healing the soul and not the body. In the case of someone working in a business, love will not be satisfied until the business is making a profit that supports the welfare of those employed, and until the heart needs of those people are met. With prostitutes in Vienna, love begins with a listening ear, a compassionate word, a loving gift, a hopeful prayer, but it will not be satisfied until women are released from the semilegal labyrinth in which some have become enmeshed.

Loving our neighbor—fellow travelers. Compared to Jesus, all are blind. None is capable of seeing the work going on in the hearts and lives of those around; only Jesus sees that. None can see into the soul of another. Blind to the all-important work of heart transformation, we cannot lead others, or we will both fall into a pit.[10]

But we can follow Jesus together. When we share with others our journey of transformation as we follow Jesus, giving a personal account of the power of Jesus in our lives, we witness to the gospel of the kingdom. The transparency of our own journey becomes a powerful testimony to others. Our best witness as the body of Christ comes when propositional truths about Jesus cause personal and corporate transformation. Jesus literally lives through us. Love prevails. When that happens, people come face-to-face with Jesus. Word and works meet. Truth and justice join hands.

GRAPPLING WITH MODERNITY, POSTMODERNITY AND NEVER-MODERN

The subject of modernity began to interest me when I started reading about postmodernity. Many of the first books I read about postmodernity were scathing. Relativism and pluralism were the new enemies, undermining the solid ground provided by modernity. But why did we think that modernity was so great?

While reading David Bosch's book *Transforming Mission*, I began to realize how deeply I had been affected by the Enlightenment and the resulting era of modernity: "The undisputed primacy of reason, . . . the substitution of the cause-effect scheme for belief in purpose, the infatuation with progress, . . . the confidence that every problem and puzzle could be solved, and the idea of the emancipated autonomous individual."[11]

Looking into a cultural mirror, I was not sure I liked what I saw.

No sooner had I begun to untangle my own beliefs from their Enlightenment roots when I realized, with a jolt, that Venezuela had never participated in the Enlightenment. Nor had China, Russia, the Philippines, India, most of Africa and countless other nations. These cultures were, in effect, very similar to postmodern cultures. Against the span of millennia, the Enlightenment itself was the exception, a 400-year bubble in world history from which some countries were now emerging, back into a world that had never experienced modernity to begin with. The effects of modernity were scattered throughout the world through colonialism, but the fundamental worldviews of much of the world's population had simply never become modern in the first place.

If I was going to be effective in making disciples among the Venezuelans, I was going to have to learn from those working in postmodern cultures.

Perhaps the idea of a proposition-only-gospel ("primacy of reason") is a luxury in the comfortable West. The vast majority of the world, more in touch with the realities of poverty, injustice, war and famine, needs a gospel far more robust. Unless the gospel speaks to these systemic issues, it has nothing to say. In postmodern society the same is true.

What does love require in a postmodern (or never-modern) society? In postmodern Europe, truth claims of any kind are suspect, and often with good reason. Consider the case of a fictional character, created by Swedish author Stieg Larsson, in his trilogy beginning with *The Girl with the Dragon Tattoo*.[12]

Larsson has an agenda: he wrote to expose the corruption of power, most notably among the rich and powerful in the government of Sweden. He shines a bright light on the inside of male-dominated power structures involved in the sex industry. The books are dark and distressing, loaded with current data about human trafficking. Although his novel is fiction, the facts he uses are not. Having been the editor of a news journal himself, Larsson was familiar with the difference between the world as it appears and as it really is.

Lisbeth Salander, one of two protagonists, is a young woman with prodigious computer skills, tattoos, piercings, a tragic family history and an attitude. Lisbeth distrusts all authority, having been repeatedly betrayed by those more powerful than she, including her parents, teachers, the police and the government institutions that tried to intervene in her upbringing. She has decided the only person she can trust is herself. Even though she only weighs ninety pounds, she learns to react and fight with lightning speed if harassed or attacked, earning her the nickname of Wasp.

Lisbeth is living in one of the most progressive, postmodern and wealthy societies on the face of the earth, but it appears to be rotting at the core. Can she trust anyone at all? Will she let her guard down for anyone? If she does, will she be hurt again? Can anyone get through to help her? Only two people get close to Lisbeth. They work beside her for months, accepting her for who she is and demonstrating disinterested concern for her as a person. Everyone else has an agenda, with Lisbeth as the object.

Here's the acid test for any disciple-making strategy in a postmodern culture: Would the strategy lead someone like Lisbeth Salander to want to become a disciple of Jesus? If the answer is no, then we had better rebalance our switches. Alone, the four propositions about Jesus, clearly stated, would never penetrate the hardened shell of someone like Lisbeth. She would not even be able to hear those propositions, true as they are, unless someone were willing to love her with disinterested love and concern, just like the other protagonist. Without that, she would never even consider following Jesus as one of his disciples. She would certainly never darken the door of a religious institution.

Most people have endured hardship in their lives, even if not as severe as Lisbeth, and every adult has some reason to distrust others. If we ever expect to see people like Lisbeth become disciples of Jesus, we must not fall into the trap of seeing them as objects for our agenda. We must never allow ourselves to think that they are targets for our mass campaign strategies. The measurements often used in the evangelical community—souls saved, church members, youth group attendees—are poison to someone like this young woman and are demeaning to anyone else.

Whether someone lives in a postmodern society or a society that never experienced modernity to begin with, relational depth and trust are the critical factors that allow someone to feel love.

What does love require in a modern society? Two drivers of modernity are technology and mass production. Underlying these is the notion that the universe is a large machine that can be understood as a complex system of cause and effect. In order for a large machine to work, a product must first be reduced to all of the component parts. Then the process for assembly is broken down into steps. If the right parts are put together in the right sequence of steps, then invariably the same product results. If the parts themselves, the number of parts necessary or the process itself can be streamlined, workers can produce the product faster, better and in greater quantities. *More, faster* and *better* become the driving values. Sociologists such as Peter Berger in *The Homeless Mind* argue that modernization is essentially "the growth and diffusion of a set of institutions rooted in the transformation of the economy by means of technology."[13]

Church and mission leaders operating under these assumptions are likely to think they can mass-produce disciples. They just need to find the right message, the right tools or the right process.

Coincidentally, they try to streamline the message and the process in order to produce disciples faster, better or in greater quantities. If these leaders hear of an organization or church that has grown in quantity, then they assume it must be the right production system and imitate it somewhere else hoping for the same results. In these mass-production strategies, the slider switch setting corresponding to propositional truth is usually very high; conversely, the one corresponding to works or justice may be sacrificed altogether. Many of the campaigns of the last century with the slogan "Reach the world in our generation" were built on these assumptions. AD 2000 was just the last of a series. None of them succeeded.

Asking what love requires is as important in a culture of modernity as in a postmodern one. Transferring information is easier to mechanize than achieving justice in an unjust situation, but alone it becomes self-defeating. People may think they are disciples, but in practical terms they may not have learned to love their neighbor. Loving one's neighbor is a messy process, unique to each individual, and cannot be put on an assembly line.

The advertising industry feeds the assembly lines by constantly researching what people value and targeting them with subtle and deceptive "good news" statements. The new car will be your ticket to freedom and power. The new hair conditioner will buy you admiration and acceptance. A new television will usher in friends and family who will enjoy one another. Viagra confers love and harmony on your marriage. Ultimately, we know these "good news" statements cannot be trusted. Cynicism has gone endemic. When the church participates in similar activities by selling truth statements without real-life connections, we simply inoculate people against Jesus.

We saw the same sort of default settings in ourselves during an internship at our home church in Michigan before leaving for Venezuela. One assignment was to lead the evangelistic outreach of the church, with a particular focus on the neighborhood. After recruiting a small group of church members, we decided to survey the neighborhood using a survey tool I had used in a class at seminary.

The survey asked several questions about the neighborhood, but the final questions asked if the people had Bibles or were interested in having a Bible study in their own home. If they said yes, then we would begin a Bible study with them. If they said no, we would thank them and carry on to the next home. The problem, as I now understand it, was not that we were offering them a Bible study. That would be a fair thing to ask anyone in the neighborhood. The problem was that we were ignoring all of the other evidence of spiritual, emotional and physical suffering that we discovered.

I wish I could go back and recalibrate my assumptions, asking what love required.

In one home, the couple was experiencing severe trauma because the husband had been in Vietnam. He couldn't get a job, he didn't know how to love his wife and he was seriously messed up on drugs. All I had to offer him was a Bible study. I wish I could go back and offer him my friendship, along with counseling for posttraumatic stress disorder, a mutual support group for his wife or temporary work from one of the businesses run by a church member. I wish I had realized that he needed far more than mental assent to four true propositions about Jesus. He needed to meet Jesus in flesh and blood, through us. Love required a whole host of possible responses, but my default settings had blinded me to many of these needs. Eventually, we ditched the survey and began talking about other ways to help the people in the neighborhood. During succeeding years, the church developed a food pantry and some other practical outreach tools in the neighborhood.

Upon our arrival in Venezuela, we carried our default settings with us. Crime and poverty were constant factors in the context where the church operated. If possible, the first thing homeowners built around their property was a high wall, preferably with bits of broken glass on top. Schools were overcrowded, and the family structure was crumbling under the combined weight of urbanization and machismo. I am deeply grieved to admit that not only did I build just as big a wall as the others, but I did not lead our church to do anything about these pervasive problems.

I preached solidly exegetical sermons. I communicated the four propositions with clarity and conviction. But beyond a few efforts to plant a tree in the median in front of our house, or to loan my tools to neighbors, we did very little to contribute practically to the community. I later heard from a missionary colleague that Tim Keller has asked the question, "If your church were to cease to exist, would the community grieve?" In our case, unfortunately, the answer was no.

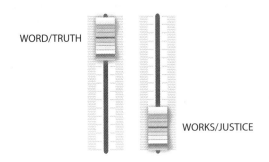

Figure 5.2. Word/truth high, works/justice low

Tim Keller is right. The body of Christ has the capacity to launch disciples of Jesus into any society, modern, postmodern or never-modern, where we can walk alongside people long enough that they will begin to wonder why someone cares that deeply about them. We can be disciples who love others without judging, without turning them into objects, welcoming them like Jesus welcomes us.

EXAMPLES OF LOVING OUR NEIGHBORS

Fortunately, many around the globe have been loving their neighbors by combining word and works, truth and justice for centuries. They have not been diverted by modernity into thinking that these can be separated.

As Rodney Stark has pointed out, Christians during the first three centuries grew because they had a better way to live. "Christian values of love and charity had, from the beginning, been translated into norms of social service and community solidarity."[14]

> To cities filled with the homeless and impoverished, Christianity offered charity as well as hope. To cities filled with newcomers and strangers, Christianity offered an immediate basis for attachments. To cities filled with orphans and widows, Christianity provided a new and expanded sense of family. To cities torn by violent ethnic strife, Christianity offered a new basis for social solidarity (cf. Pelikan 1987:21). And to cities faced with epidemics, fires and earthquakes, Christianity offered effective nursing services.[15]

Throughout the world, missionaries have been at the forefront of caring for the needs of the people around them. The Irish missionaries in the fifth century were the ones who laid the foundations of modern Europe.[16] The ones who stayed to nurse the sick during the Black Plague were the Christians. William Carey broke open the door for missions from Europe and North America when he began literacy campaigns, hospitals, orphanages and more.

Working openly together to address community issues. The organization Community Health Evangelism, commonly known as CHE, has a wonderful philosophy of community development.[17] When they enter a community, they make no secret of their faith. They will tell community leaders, "We are followers of Jesus, and Jesus told us to love our neighbor as ourselves. That is why we are here. Now, what are the issues that you are facing in your community, and how can we help?" From that moment on, every single thing they do reflects on Jesus—what he would do, how he would act.

They tell stories about common problems, inviting the community leaders to discuss the stories, listening to discover if those problems are on the minds of the leaders. If they are, then the members of CHE offer training for local volunteers to deal with the specific needs. Conversations about Jesus arise naturally as they work with the volunteers.

But imagine what would happen if they were to enter the community without saying why they were there. The community leaders would be suspicious of a hidden agenda. When a conversation comes up in which the missionary mentions Jesus, it is too late. To the wary, they have been the victims of "bait and switch" and the trust vanishes. "Aha," they will say, "we knew you were hiding something."

Keeping the faith. If one were to delete from the world all that Christians have done to love their neighbors through combining word and works, or truth and justice, it would be appalling. In 2008 a reporter wrote an article for the *Times* in which he recognized this fact, even though he was a confessed atheist.

> Now a confirmed atheist, I've become convinced of the enormous contribution that Christian evangelism makes in Africa: sharply distinct from the work of secular NGOs, government projects and international aid efforts. These alone will not do. Education and training alone will not do. In Africa Christianity changes people's hearts. It brings a spiritual transformation. The rebirth is real. The change is good.
>
> I used to avoid this truth by applauding—as you can—the practical work of mission churches in Africa. It's a pity, I would say, that salvation is part of the package, but Christians black and white, working in Africa, do heal the sick, do teach people to read and write; and only the severest kind of secularist could see a mission hospital or school and say the world would be better without it. I would allow that if faith was needed to motivate missionaries to help, then, fine: but what counted was the help, not the faith.

But this doesn't fit the facts. Faith does more than support the missionary; it is also transferred to his flock. This is the effect that matters so immensely, and which I cannot help observing.[18]

When truth and justice walk hand in hand, even an atheist can't help but notice.

Mobilizing missional communities. Approximately three hundred missional communities operate in and around Sheffield, England. Missional communities consist of fifty to seventy people who make a practice of eating together, listening to short testimonies or messages, discussing God's Word and praying. Then they pray and plan how to improve their community in the name of Jesus.

Missional communities run food pantries, clean up streets and visit local hospitals, doing what God leads them to do. One missional community runs a toddlers' group where parents receive support, do crafts together and sing songs with their children, pointing everyone to God. Another missional community cleaned up the garden of a local pub, and then the pub offered to let them use the grounds for a youth group. The impact of these missional communities has drawn the attention of political leaders, now working together with them for the common good.

Rolling up your sleeves and getting involved. Like any big city in the United States, the city of Memphis has long endured racial struggles. Several years ago, one of the leaders of the First Presbyterian Church had a conversation with an African American woman in the city. She asked him when he was going to roll up his sleeves and get involved. That conversation eventually contributed to the Shalom Project. The mission of the Memphis Shalom Project is "to serve the City of Memphis by mobilizing the church to leverage its resources to transform our most distressed neighborhoods through the local church."[19]

Shalom is a rich biblical word. These church leaders of Memphis understood it to mean "spiritual health and the church, public safety, family life, education, health, housing and neighborhood revitalization, economic development, community involvement, and arts and education."[20] They defined 127 neighborhood zones within the city, and then, applying census data, determined that thirty-seven zones were considered vulnerable and fifty-six were distressed and needed significant help to restore *shalom* to those neighborhoods. The Shalom Project has created a mechanism whereby churches, nonprofit agencies and the city can work together to help distressed neighborhoods.

The Shalom Project is working to influence the city for good. With two thousand churches, two hundred parachurch agencies, six synagogues and four mosques, all of which want to help, they have created the mechanisms for disciples of Jesus to respond to the question, What does love require?

In Memphis, truth and justice walk hand in hand, doing what love requires.

Caring for the oppressed. In the drug trade, Mexico is known as a trampoline, receiving drugs and then bouncing them on to the lucrative market in the north. During the 1990s, drug runners from South America decided that it would be easier to give middlemen in Mexico a cut of the drugs as payment in lieu of cash. Before that time, few Mexicans were users. With this strategic shift, however, the only way to convert the drugs into cash was to sell it on the local market. Cheap drugs flooded Mexico. Many became addicted, particularly men.

One of our colleagues remembers asking a young neighbor boy how many men on his block were *not* drug users. The boy thought for a few minutes, pointed at the missionary and said, "You." Between skyrocketing rates of drug addiction and the already existing problems of alcoholism, marriages came under increasing stress, often leading to domestic abuse.

One day a woman arrived at the door of colleagues of ours, fleeing from her husband who was trying to kill her. Steve and Lois put her up, fed her and eventually found a hidden apartment where she could live. She was not alone. Slowly other abused women discovered this place of refuge, and thus began a constant stream of women. Women from the local churches would care for them, loving them and their children. Soon, after coming into contact with the loving body of Christ, the women began to relax and then to flourish in the environment of love and protection, becoming interested in what these *evangélicos* believed. Many started attending the church service, and eventually some husbands came to Jesus as well. After several years, the safe house had to close because the location has been compromised. Steve said that during the time it was operating, no other ministry of the church had been as powerful in drawing people to Jesus as the women's shelter.

We should not be surprised. God is the one who said that he, the Lord, "executes justice for the oppressed . . . gives food to the hungry . . . sets the prisoners free . . . opens the eyes of the blind . . . raises up those who are bowed down . . . loves the righteous . . . protects the strangers . . . supports the fatherless and the widow, but . . . thwarts the way of the wicked" (Psalm 146:7-9).

DISCIPLES ASK WHAT LOVE REQUIRES

Each person on the face of the planet, young or old, anorexic or obese, short or tall, beautiful or ugly, black or white, straight or gay, tattooed or not, is a person created by God, whom God loves with abandon and for whom the Son of God died. Our job is to extend that kind of love to one another, to our neighbors and to our enemies.

As we listen and obey, working together with love and unity, God will open up channels for his love to flow to others, touching lives, redeeming the darkness and giving us opportunity to invite others to join us as his disciples.

Disciples Make Disciples

Preaching and Group Interaction

Make disciples of all the nations.

MATTHEW 28:19

The large auditorium filled up quickly. We were visiting a worship service of New Life Church on the campus of the Illinois Institute of Technology. A young woman with Down syndrome met us as we walked in, greeted us warmly, took our hands and helped us find seats. We enjoyed good preaching, warm singing and, to our delight, witnessed the baptism of several people.

A portable tank sat below the stage. The tank had been designed with a shelf for the baptismal candidate to sit on with his or her feet in the water at one end. Lying back on the shelf would cover him or her completely with water. The process was simple and effective. No special training was required.

Before being baptized, the new believers told their stories of coming to Christ. But the pastor did not officiate. Instead, two people from the congregation stood on either side, baptizing the new believer. One was the man or woman who had been most influential in bringing the new person to faith. The other was the leader of the small group to which he or she belonged. As each new believer professed his or her faith in Jesus, the two who performed the baptism publicly accepted their responsibility to walk alongside the new disciple.

The principle is very simple: disciples make disciples.

During my tenure as the director of TEAM, some well-intentioned changes sparked significant resistance. One person in particular opposed the changes, attacking me personally. Because of the nature of the situation, I was unable to defend myself. I felt alone, afraid and discouraged. At the peak of the emotional maelstrom, our pastor preached from the book of Daniel. During the sermon, it was as if God himself looked straight at me, speaking through the pastor, "O man who is loved very much, do not be afraid. May peace be with you. Be strong and have strength of heart" (Dan 10:19 NLV). I don't know if anyone else was moved by those words, but for me they were a lifeline. Jesus knew me and my circumstances. He reassured me that I was, indeed, following him—the decision I had made enjoyed his blessing. In that moment, I grew to know Jesus better and was strengthened in my relationship to him as his disciple.

The pastor and I also enjoyed a personal relationship and managed, in spite of our busy schedules, to get together for breakfast every couple months to talk about life. He listened to my story, encouraged me and helped me find my way through the confusion. Over the following weeks and months, the fog slowly lifted and the situation began to resolve. Between the truth of God's Word and the counsel of a godly friend, I was able to stay the course and see the Lord work in some unusual ways.

When two or three people gather together to discern and carry out God's will in the light of the teaching of God's Word, his will gets done. Disciples make disciples.

Our small group from church met one evening, and I suggested that each tell of two or three shaping moments in our lives. We listened with great interest as each shared unique, life-changing stories, many of which were Spirit-filled examples of life transformation. Afterward, someone made the comment that not one of those shaping incidents took place during or because of a sermon. After lighthearted laughter, someone asked, "So why do we spend so much time listening to preaching?"

Stories like those we shared with each other make us who we are, creating a memorable record of growth in our spiritual lives. The shared stories reinforce our sense of belonging to the family of God. Sometimes they occur during sermons, as with me on that memorable day, but often they occur in the company of others.

Earlier, I proposed a definition of *disciples* as those who are learning of Jesus, following Jesus and loving like Jesus, together, for a lifetime. We become his disciples the moment we begin this process of learning, following and loving, and the process continues every hour of every day of our lives.

Making disciples is the process of encouraging others to learn, follow and love him so that they can join the family and grow in their relationship with him as members of his family. How we do that is often a reflection of the cultural context in which we grow up.

In this set of cultural slider switches, one switch corresponds to the degree to which one's church or one's ministry team uses Bible studies,

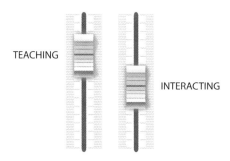

TEACHING

INTERACTING

Figure 6.1. Teaching and interacting

lectures or preaching to make disciples, and the opposite but yoked switch corresponds to the degree to which the church uses mentoring and group relationships to make disciples. Both are important, but if one or the other is too high or too low, the dynamic tension is lost and our capacity and effectiveness at making disciples is diminished.

MAINTAINING BIBLICAL TENSION:
TEACHING AND INTERACTING

Peter preached a resounding sermon on the day of Pentecost with amazing results,[1] and Jesus preached unforgettable sermons.[2] Paul gave his testimony several times to large audiences, and taught through the night in Ephesus.[3] But these examples of expositing the truth seem to have been the exception rather than the rule.

Much disciple making seemed to occur through discussion and interaction. When Jesus preached to the crowd about the kingdom,[4] "The disciples came to him and asked, 'Why do you speak to the people in parables?'" (Mt 13:10 NIV). Jesus answered their question by giving them more to think about, distinguishing them from the crowd that listened but could not hear, that saw but could not perceive. This was the disciple-making process in action: taking a truth preached to the crowd, then helping the disciples understand the implications for their lives.

Jesus knew when they needed another dose of truth, and when they needed to interact with him or each other. When circumstances occurred that the disciples did not understand, he would lead them back to the truth of the Word. He constantly adjusted and readjusted his approach to help them mature as his disciples.

Paul's letter to the Ephesians constitutes a superlative sermon on the nature of the body of Christ. To have been in a gathering of fellow disciples at the time and to hear someone read this letter—from beginning to end—must have been life changing. The entire letter is packed with information.

But as he writes, Paul clearly states that the mechanisms for moving forward as growing disciples belonged to the whole body:

> But speaking the truth in love, *we* are to grow up in all aspects into Him, who is the head, even Christ, from whom the *whole body*, being fitted and held together by *what every joint supplies*, according to the proper working of *each individual part*, causes the growth of the body for the building up of itself in love. . . . Therefore . . . speak truth *each one of you* with his neighbor, for we are members of one another. (Eph 4:15-16, 25)

Truth is certainly important, and theological truth possibly the most important, but every disciple involved in a mutual disciple-making process is entrusted with the responsibility of speaking the truth in love to one another. The "growth of the body" is the responsibility of everyone.

John Stott, in his book *Between Two Worlds*,[5] explored the idea of a metaphorical bridge between two worlds: the biblical world (text, history and ancient culture) and the world in which all of us live our everyday lives (current happenings, relationships, culture and circumstances). He encouraged anyone involved in preaching to be diligent in studying and understanding both worlds in order to build a bridge between them. Stott feared that seminary students would develop expertise in the biblical world of truth without equal expertise in the world of daily life, and would, in effect, remain fixed on one side of the bridge.

Interaction between disciples, in contrast with preaching, is naturally rooted in daily life and moves across the same metaphorical bridge, but in the other direction. Disciple-making groups have the capacity to face life's unruly circumstances together, then seek the truth and wisdom of the biblical world to apply to that unique situation.

Just as sermons without application fail to cross the bridge from one direction, disciple-making relationships, mentoring or small groups can also fail to cross the bridge in the other direction, never arriving at the truth of God's Word.

In my moment of leadership crisis, a sermon connected exactly and perfectly with what I was going through, crossing the bridge and arriving directly into my context. At other times dozens if not hundreds of sermons simply did not touch the need of the moment. If preaching is the foremost method of disciple making, people may come and go on a Sunday morning with the personal heartache or individual need undiscovered and unmet. Preaching was never intended to carry the whole load of disciple making.

This bridge runs in both directions. One-way communication through preaching or teaching must be held in balance with interaction and discussion between disciples. The slider switches must move in dynamic tension with one another.

HIGH AND LOW CONTEXTS—CULTURAL COMMUNICATION CHALLENGES

Related to this set of slider switches is the degree to which one's cultural context influences communication and decision making. Context includes "the subject or activity, the situation, one's status in a social system, past experience, and culture."[6]

> A high-context (HC) communication or message is one in which most of the information is either in the physical context or internalized in the person, while very little is in the coded, explicit, transmitted part of the message. A low-context (LC) communication is just the opposite; i.e., the mass of the information is vested in the explicit code.[7]

In a low-context culture, written or spoken words have value in and of themselves, without reference to the situation, speaker, status or past experience. A high-context culture depends on a wide variety of cultural, relational and nonverbal clues.

Cultures have widely varying assumptions about the importance of context. If a businessperson from the United States goes to China to sign a contract with a Chinese counterpart, she is likely to be confused by the amount of time invested in eating, chatting, finding mutual relations and sharing of personal information—a high-context cultural situation. The American may be frustrated because she wants to get to the business at hand. The Chinese person, however, wants to know if he can trust the American, and wants to understand more of the context from which that person comes. Once they have established trust, signing the documents may be a simple matter of five minutes at the end of the shared meal.

By contrast, if the Chinese businessperson comes to the United States, he may find himself seated at a table with a lawyer, his business counterpart and a written contract he is expected to sign. He is entering a low-context situation in which he may know little or nothing of the status of the other person and has no experience or acquaintance in common. In this case, the Chinese businessperson will be frustrated because he does not have enough information about the context to make a good decision. The American, however, wants to get the document signed, avoiding unnecessary chitchat.

As with other cultural slider switches, navigating the tension between these extremes is important for disciples. New Life Church has developed a high-context culture in which the new disciple is taught, encouraged and challenged through interaction with others, while at the same time hearing the truth taught every Sunday.

According to research on conversion to Mormonism carried out by Rodney Stark, conversion happens when the relational connections with one group of people become stronger than those of another group. According to his research, only one in one thousand converted through cold calls or contact with complete strangers, a low-context situation. In contrast, one out of two converted among those who had a relational connection to someone who was already a Mormon, a high-context situation.[8] The actual doctrines of the Mormon church mattered later, after the people had converted and become Mormons.

In 1996, I joined 55,000 other men at a meeting of Promise Keepers held in Chicago's Soldier Field. That evening, the speaker asked everyone who had become a follower of Jesus through mass evangelism to stand up. Some people stood up, and looking carefully, I could see a couple here or an individual there. Then the presenter made the same request of all those who had come to Christ because someone—a friend, family member or neighbor—had taken a personal interest in them. A loud "whoomp" of sound arose as what appeared to be 55,000 men stood to their feet. The presenter pointed out the importance of bridges of friendship and relationship if others are going to come to Christ.

Both the illustration taken from the research on conversion to Mormonism and the story from Promise Keepers demonstrate that people are much more likely to make a change in a high-context situation.

Dependence on low-context approaches to disciple making, such as cold call evangelism, preaching, lecturing or fill-in-the-blank notebooks, may be due partly to a penchant for mass production, a corollary to low-context culture. Mass production involves analyzing things and breaking them down into their individual parts, then creating a mechanistic step-by-step process for assembly. When followed precisely, people can mass-produce automobiles, coffeemakers and computers. Producing a car, however, assumes that the raw material is static and does not change.

But disciples are people, and no two people are the same. People differ from culture to culture, within the same culture, within the same tribe or clan, and even week to week. Humans come with a wide variety of issues attached and will probably resist being put through the same mold as everyone else. One person may have a life-threatening addiction, another might have a physical illness, the next a relationship boondoggle with his family, the next a learning disability. The person who has none of these probably does not realize that he or she is dealing with issues of pride or intolerance of those who do.

Disciple making must meet these people right where they are and help them take the next step in following Jesus. A powerful sermon may touch 10 to 15 percent of the people in the audience, but what about the other 85 percent? What about all of the issues they are facing? Disciples cannot be mass-produced.

Ministry teams often use Bible studies as the primary way of attracting interested people or helping new believers grow. In the early stages of a new church, these Bible studies may take place with one or two people and move naturally into a high-context setting. If the Bible study is effective and the interested person makes a decision to follow Christ, then he or she will probably be invited to attend a Sunday morning worship service that includes a lecture/sermon. As more people join, the leaders will likely move more and more to a lecture format. What begins as high-context gradually slides into a low-context approach.

For a ministry team to work well together, the members will have to identify and share with one another what their personal default settings are, and then together they will need to decide on a course of action that reflects biblical tension between one-way preaching or teaching and two-way interacting.

EXAMPLES OF DISCIPLES MAKING DISCIPLES

Empowering every disciple. Some amazing disciple-making movements are occurring around the world today. Jerry Trousdale of CityTeam and David Garrison of IMB have been researching sixty-two such movements.[9] A striking feature of many of these movements is how quickly new believers are empowered to go out and make disciples themselves. Some of these movements are using Bible stories, or chronological storytelling, to make disciples. In the method known as Training for Trainers (T4T), they do not let new disciples leave their meetings without first practicing what they are going to say and do when they meet others.[10]

As Rodney Stark discovered, the people who are best situated to make disciples are those who already have networks of relationships of people whom they know. When those people are empowered to share their personal stories of meeting Jesus, they have far more influence than the preacher who is not known.

Intentionally building connections with coaches and mentors. New Life Church knows that any new believer has a long way to go to become an effective disciple, and they make sure he or she is connected to people who will provide coaching and mentoring along the way.

A musician cannot learn to play a musical instrument or sing well without practice and without feedback from a teacher. Music certainly involves the transfer of information, and students hear lectures on the history of music and music theory. But little Jamie cannot play the flute, violin or trombone without actually trying. The results at first

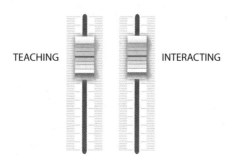

TEACHING   INTERACTING

Figure 6.2. Teaching high, interacting high

might be excruciating, but with feedback from a coach or mentor, he gradually improves through practice. The process is instructive. Play, listen, evaluate (usually with the help of a teacher), decide what to do to improve, then play again. And again. And again. Feedback from the teacher, especially important in the beginning stages, helps Jamie develop good habits and become a good musician.

Likewise with learning sports. Despite literature and lectures on the theory of basketball, soccer and the intricate strategies of baseball, the game begins when players put on their uniforms, step onto the field and put the ball in play. Only after throwing, kicking or hitting the ball a few thousand times, with the constant feedback of a coach, will the player begin to predict with accuracy what will happen the next time he or she throws, kicks or hits the ball. Professional football players, basketball players, baseball players and golfers still work out with the help of a coach.

Practicing transparency. When I was young, our family moved to a summer location in Pakistan. The process involved packing a lot of suitcases and equipment onto a trailer, delivering it to the train station, then embarking on a train going north from Lahore to Rawalpindi. Early in the morning, Dad was busily trying to pack everything, experiencing all the frustrations of "too much stuff and too little space" compounded by not enough time. I was an excited ten-year-old, a boy without any responsibilities, bouncing around, making a nuisance of myself. At one point I directly disobeyed something Dad said and, in his frustration, he slapped me across the face. Normally, he was very systematic and never disciplined in anger. I knew, however, what I had done wrong and quickly retreated.

We arrived at the train station on time, transferred all of the luggage, and soon the train rumbled out of the station northward. An hour or two later, as I was sitting in one of the compartments with other young people, Dad came into the car with his Bible in his hands and asked to speak with me. When we were alone, he apologized for slapping me. He said that he should not have done what he did. He said he was sorry, and then he asked me to forgive him. I was astounded. Dad, asking me, to forgive him. I did. Since then I have heard sermons and read books with the theme of forgiveness, but no sermon ever had the powerful effect of that one moment in real life, when one disciple (my dad) humbly asked another disciple (extremely immature me) for forgiveness. Throughout life, whenever I have needed to ask or give forgiveness, I have been able to do so, all because of that life lesson from a valued mentor, my father, who practiced transparency with me.

In a high-context situation, like our home, transparently admitting failure provided a powerful example to imitate.

Recruiting a mentor. Faced with overwhelming responsibilities as the director of TEAM, God provided a former leader of another mission organization who lived in our area to be my mentor. As we shared our journeys, we developed a mutual disciple-making relationship with one another. Every four to six weeks I met with him for breakfast, talked through what I was facing, interacted, reflected and reacted. Every time we met, I left with a clearer idea of what to improve or change about my performance as a leader. We often talked about theory and books, exchanging information continually, but the transformative effect of our conversations kept us searching for the right thing to do, desiring to obey Jesus in a world of choices.

Forming breakout groups. In 2004, I helped to organize a conference for approximately two hundred of TEAM's global leaders. I invited the pastor of our church to give the Bible messages, and the worship team from the church led the worship times. We decided that we would have approximately a half hour of worship and singing, followed by a half hour of teaching, but then, for another thirty minutes, we would ask everyone to move their chairs into groups of three to four people to discuss a few questions related to the message, taking time to pray for one another.

We had rebalanced the slider switch controlling information delivery with the switch that controlled interaction and discussion among the participants.

Starting huddles. Many churches have shifted the burden of individual disciple making to the small group, or the home group. Too often, however, the home group adopts the most familiar pattern, which is yet another Bible or book study in which we "listen" to the equivalent of a written lecture. The basic setting of the slider switches remains the same, with the side corresponding to lecturing and preaching set high and the side corresponding to mentoring or group discussion, where accountability can happen, set very low.

In a "huddle,"[11] six to eight participants regularly respond to the question, "What has the Lord said to you recently?" The entire group, with access to Scripture and to the Spirit, can be relied upon to confirm or not confirm the answer to the question, creating a mutual account-ability group. Biblical understanding and theological information are brought into the framework of obedience. Instead of beginning with the Word and working toward a sometimes distant application, this question begins with the application, then uses the Word, the com-munity of faith and prayer to confirm the validity of that application. Disciples are making disciples.

Learning from others on the journey. In the early 1980s, my wife and I had started to work in Caña de Azúcar, a government-subsidized subdivision of Maracay, Venezuela. We had purchased half of a duplex, and in order to accommodate our family and what I hoped would be a new body of believers, we began an extensive remodeling project. My formal training was in music and theology, but for this project I had to learn how to lay concrete block, weld I-beams and build cabinets.

Bill, a fellow missionary with experience in construction, lived a couple hours away. I asked him if he would be willing to give me advice from time to time and show me how to do what I needed to do. He quickly realized that I was going to need more than advice. I was going to need some actual hands-on training. At considerable sacrifice to himself, his family and the work he was already doing, he drove over and helped me two days a week for several months. I was humbled and grateful.

When we laid our first course of cement block, he showed me how to mix the mortar, how to put in enough water for the proper consistency, how to string the line, how to lay the block on the mortar and squeeze it down to the proper height. I did not know it then, but I had successfully recruited my first mentor. I learned a lot about construction, and about six months later we moved into our new home. But what I learned as we talked was far more significant.

One day as we were working together, he asked me a question: "Charlie, how many of the people who contribute to your ministry are wealthy people?" I thought it through, mentally running down the list of the various people who were generously and graciously contributing to our financial support. I knew of one such person, but she had quickly diminished her contributions so that by the time we were talking, I could say, "No one." Then he asked, "How many are poor people?" That was easier. "No one," I said.

He responded, "Well, see there? Seems to me that the global missionary work force is being carried on the backs of the middle class. I've asked that question of other people, and they all answer it the same way." Then he asked me another question: "How many middle-class churches do we have in Venezuela?" I thought through what I knew of the 160-plus churches among whom TEAM worked at the time and answered, "Not very many." He responded, "How will we ever see the churches of Venezuela develop their missionary-sending enterprise if there are so few churches among the middle class?"

Bill was not a missiologist; he was a fellow disciple who was sharing his journey with me. He was not trying to compare rates of urbanization around the globe, nor make categorical statements about mission strategy. Neither of us knew at the time that Venezuela, at 79 percent,[12] had one of the highest rates of urbanization in the world, or that by 1990, a short decade later, it would be 88 percent.[13] Having just moved his family to a middle-class section of Caracas in obedience to the Lord's leading, he was simply sharing his thoughts.

The Lord used that conversation to set the direction for my life for the next twenty years. His questions and comments continued to reverberate in my mind for years to come. My wife and I moved to the capital city of Caracas to help begin a new church among middle-class Venezuelans. We recruited fifteen other missionaries to help us. We encouraged others in Venezuela to take on the challenge of the cities, and I included urbanization in my PhD work.

All of those subsequent decisions were guided by prayer and the Word of God, but God used a simple conversation with a fellow disciple, laying block on a sweaty, sun-soaked day in Maracay, Venezuela, to guide our lives. Bill showed me the power of a mentoring relationship as a fellow pilgrim willing to share his journey with me.

Developing relationships across age boundaries. Our son Evan works as the youth minister in an evangelical church in the Episcopal tradition. Among other areas, he is responsible for the confirmation classes. Early on, he realized that if he could recruit adults from the congregation to meet regularly with the students during the months of confirmation classes, he would accomplish far more than if he just taught the material himself. He continued to teach the curriculum, but he increasingly involved adults as mentors for the students. On confirmation Sunday, the mentor stands with him to hand the newly confirmed members their certificates. Those relationships, developed in a few months, have the potential of continuing for a lifetime. Rebalancing the switches in this required program has given new life to the youth ministry of the church and has increased the active participation of the adults.

DISCIPLES MAKE DISCIPLES

Every disciple has the capacity to help another disciple in the journey of following and obeying Jesus. Whether it happens while sharing the journey and talking, or in a formal confirmation class, every lesson someone learns can be passed on to someone else.

Those who were baptized at New Life Church that Sunday knew that if they brought someone else to Christ, they would have the responsibility of walking with the new believer. Someday they would be standing before the congregation, accepting responsibility for a newly baptized believer. No wonder this church has multiplied into more than twenty locations in and around the Chicago area.[14]

We cannot rely on preaching or teaching alone, as important as those are. A good sermon does not make disciples. Disciples make disciples.

Leaders Equip
Disciples for Ministry

Equippers and Ministers

*For the equipping of the saints
for the work of service.*

Ephesians 4:12

The church we helped start in the city of Maracay, Venezuela, grew rapidly. People were growing in relationship with one another, and several were involved in running the programs. Our home assignment was approaching, however, and my wife and I would be gone for a full year. We needed to have ongoing leadership in the church while we were gone, but how? The traditional approach was to ask another missionary to carry my responsibilities for the year we were gone. None were available.

During seminary, I had been introduced to the book *Missionary Methods: St. Paul's or Ours?* by Roland Allen. In this prescient book, written a century ago, he challenges the assumption that new believers are not capable of carrying out ministry in the power of the Holy Spirit.

If the first converts are taught to depend upon the missionary, if all work, evangelistic, educational, social is concentrated in his hands, the infant community learns to rest passively upon the man from whom they receive their first insight into the Gospel. Their faith, having no sphere for its growth and development, lies dormant. A tradition very rapidly grows up that nothing can be done without the authority and guidance of the missionary, the people wait for him to move, and the longer they do so, the more incapable they become of any independent action. *Thus the leader is confirmed in the habit of gathering all authority into his own hands, and of despising the powers of his people, until he makes their inactivity an excuse for denying their capacity.* The fatal mistake has been made of teaching the converts to rely upon the wrong source of strength. Instead of seeking it in the working of the Holy Spirit in themselves, they seek it in the missionary. They put him in the place of Christ, they depend on him.[1] [Emphasis added]

With these powerful words ringing in my mind, I set out to recruit three potential leaders to preach, lead worship, study Scripture and learn spiritual decision making together. One young man, Antonio, studied computer programming in the prestigious Simón Bolívar University in Caracas. Another, Pablo, studied at the nearby seminary, and a third, Sergio, taught in a grade school. In rotation each Sunday, one of us would take a turn preaching and another leading the worship. On Wednesday nights we met halfway between Caracas and Maracay at a park near the highway, folding table, chairs and kerosene lantern in hand.

Together, we evaluated the message and the worship of the previous Sunday. (I knew we were making progress when they began to critique my sermons as energetically as they critiqued each other's.) We studied the Scripture for the following Sunday, giving the person who would speak ideas on his presentation. We talked through organizational issues. We prayed. Praying, laughing, studying, slapping bugs, encouraging one another—the Lord met with us and smiled. When Kris and I left for our home assignment, the church moved forward without a hitch. When we returned from home assignment, the pastoral team carried on, and within a year we took our next assignment in Caracas.

I was pleased that I had worked myself out of a job and had successfully trained a select few to exercise their gifts in leadership. I did not realize until much later that I did not create a pattern in which everyone in the church learned to use their gifts. I had succeeded in bypassing the traditional requirement of hiring an outsider; I had multiplied myself threefold. By inviting Antonio, a computer programmer, and Sergio, a schoolteacher, to join the pastoral team, I had shown that a person did not have to be paid clergy to do ministry. But I did not succeed in developing a culture in which everyone there learned to exercise their gifts in ministry. Approximately 85 percent of the people were still happy just to attend on Sunday morning.

I had partially applied the principle: leaders equip disciples to minister.

The slider switches paired in this case are leaders on one side, and disciples who minister on the other. When leaders lead but do not equip disciples to minister, the leader switch is set high and the disciple as minister switch is very low. When disciples minister, but are not equipped, that switch is set high and the leader switch is low. For the church to move forward in a healthy way, leaders equip disciples who minister and quickly become leaders who equip others.

MAINTAINING BIBLICAL TENSION: EQUIPPERS AND MINISTERS

The premier passage that speaks to this dynamic occurs in Ephesians:

> He gave some as apostles, and some as prophets, and some as evangelists, and some as pastors and teachers, for the *equipping*

of the saints for the work of service, to the building up of the body of Christ; until we all attain to the unity of the faith, and of the knowledge of the Son of God, to a mature man, to the measure of the stature which belongs to the fullness of Christ. (Eph 4:11-13)

Apostles, prophets, evangelists, teachers and pastors only succeed when they have discovered, empowered, trained, equipped and released everyone else into ministry. They do *not* succeed when they only exercise their gifts themselves, even if they are very, very good at what they do. God provides every gift necessary for the body as a whole to function. Leaders are responsible to find, empower and equip others to function using the gifts given to them for the good of the body.

Everyone, not just a few. A person sitting quietly in the gatherings of the body who does not know how to effectively participate in ministry is a sign of leadership failure. I was happy with three men involved in ministry and considered myself something of an example. But what about all the others who did not know how to use their own gifts in ministry?

Paul's directive in Ephesians has received considerable attention since 2000. Alan Hirsch, in his book *Permanent Revolution*,[2] makes a strong case that every disciple of Jesus has been given at least one of five basic gifts listed in Ephesians. In *Building a Discipleship Culture*,[3] Mike Breen calls these gifts the base gifts of the church.

If this is true, then everyone who becomes a disciple is *potentially* gifted as a teacher, pastor, evangelist, prophet or apostle. Those who are leading are responsible to discover others who have those gifts and then invite them to exercise their gifts in ministry, coaching them until they are effective. Ultimately, these new ministers will find others whom they can equip, becoming leaders themselves. Paul refers to these five gifts as those that are primarily responsible for equipping the rest of the body.

True, the Bible contains three lists of gifts given to members of the body,[4] and the five gifts mentioned in Ephesians are only one list. The book of Ephesians, however, is considered the *magna carta* of the church, and though these five are certainly not the only gifts, the combination of these particular gifts in a leadership team creates an unstoppable dynamic.

Leaders with apostolic and evangelistic gifting will constantly be looking outward, pointing beyond to those who have not yet been reached with the good news. Those with teaching and pastoral gifting will constantly be looking inward to build depth of understanding and love among those who are disciples. Those with prophetic gifting will be quick to ponder what God thinks on the matter. If only the pastors and teachers are leading, everyone will be content but the church will go nowhere. If the apostles and evangelists predominate, the church can easily blow apart. The interplay of all is necessary for the health of the body.

Health, not size. Size is not the best metric for health, whether considering the human body or the body of Christ. What determines health is whether all systems are working correctly, in cooperation with one another—each cell doing its part within that system. The cardiovascular, skeletal, muscular, digestive and nervous systems are similar to the five basic systems that have to operate within the church. Apostles point the way forward, pastors function in harmony with teachers, both work closely with evangelists in cooperation with prophets. A single cell is ineffective on its own, but as leaders equip others the systems grow and develop in harmony with one another.

Imagine what would happen if churches assembled leadership teams of people who represented all five of these gifts, and each leader began looking for disciples with those gifts to mentor and equip them. Those with pastoral gifting would look for others with pastoral gifting and train and equip them. Those with evangelistic gifting would equip others eager to learn, and so forth. Leaders would be those who had grown in their abilities and spiritual effectiveness in using these gifts, and who would find and inspire others to follow in their footsteps as they followed the Lord.

Small groups or ministry teams could form with these five gifts in mind, each functioning as the body, learning to discern and carry out God's will together. Each person could develop the gifts he or she had been given and grow in ministry by exercising those gifts in the home, neighborhood, small group and workplace. The body would constantly be moving outward into every sphere of life and work.

How many potential apostles, prophets, evangelists, teachers and pastors are listening on Sunday morning wondering what to do next? Imagine the explosive growth and multiplication of the church in Maracay if we had identified all those with these five gifts, and if we had trained and mobilized them to find and equip others. Everyone would have been involved in ministry, and the impact on the church and on the surrounding community could have been awesome.

Roles, not positions. Paul is not describing positions in an organizational chart. He is not talking about institutional structures that imbue some with power and authority. He is talking about the essential roles that must exist for the body to be healthy. The first disciples had a hard time learning this, and it seems not much has changed.

On the last walk to Jerusalem, when Jesus announced to his disciples that he would be crucified, they immediately began to argue about who would have the most important positions in the kingdom.[5] Jesus patiently explained that in the kingdom the greatest are those who serve. A few short days later, after he had shared the last Passover meal with them and his heart was breaking, even then "a dispute arose among them as to which of them was considered to be greatest" (Lk 22:24 NIV). The more imminent his death, the more the question of succession arose.

Why is this lesson so hard to learn? How did we end up with churches that have a cadre of special people with titles that set them apart, in some cases almost usurping the position that belongs only to God? Jesus clearly tells us that we are to call no one our *father* except our Father in heaven, and we are not to let anyone call us *Rabbi* or *Leader.* "But do not be called Rabbi; for One is your Teacher, and you are all brothers. Do not call anyone on earth your father; for One is your Father, He who is in heaven. Do not be called leaders; for One is your Leader, that is, Christ" (Mt 23:8-10).

Service, not power. One way to test whether we are thinking of gifting for service or hierarchical positions is to ask, "Do women have pastoral gifts?" Many will answer that probably more women have pastoral gifts than men. But as soon as someone asks, "Can a woman be *the* pastor?" turning it into a title, then the issue becomes power and control. Suddenly the Scripture passages about women assume disproportionate importance—are women allowed to exercise authority? If so, how much? But Jesus said that power and control were precisely the opposite of what he intended, didn't he? If all the women with pastoral gifts were equipped, empowered and released into the body and into our neighborhoods, imagine the healing effect.

Many people do not take this passage in Ephesians seriously, afraid of abuses by those who take on these titles. We need to be clear: control and abuse are diametrically opposite to what Jesus said: "The greatest among you will be your servant. For those who exalt themselves will be humbled, and those who humble themselves will be exalted" (Mt 23:11-12 NIV). The intent of the apostolic gift is not to control others, but to show them the way and help them find it. Those who function with the pastoral gift do so with the intent of lovingly coming alongside people and demonstrating the presence of Jesus in the midst of their journey.

Others sidestep the power issue by saying that the gifts of apostle and prophet no longer exist. According to this argument, these gifts only existed in the beginning and then were no longer given. Apostles who were eyewitnesses and were called to write the Scriptures are, indeed, a class by themselves. Some apostles were given the assignment to write the Scripture, but that does not mean that only those who wrote Scripture could be apostles. Clearly the Bible mentions apostles who were not authors.

If God no longer gives apostolic or prophetic gifting to the church, why not assume the same thing about the other gifts—teaching, preaching or evangelism? Or conversely, as Hirsch asks, "If we allow the titles of Pastor and Teacher, why should we deny the titles of Apostle, Prophet, and Evangelist?"[6]

HIGH AND LOW POWER DISTANCE—CULTURAL LEADERSHIP CHALLENGES

"The degree of perfection required is in direct proportion to the distance from the audience." The speaker in this case was not an anthropologist, missiologist or guru on leadership development, but an accomplished musician. He went on: "If little Suzy is going to play her flute in the living room of her house, surrounded by family, she can make several mistakes and everyone will clap and cheer nonetheless. If she is playing in a recital in the school auditorium, she can make a few mistakes, and the audience will still enjoy her performance. If she is on the radio, with an infinite distance to the audience, she has to be perfect."[7]

The distance from the audience is an important factor for developing leaders as well. When disciples gather in cells or households, everyone can use their gifts in service to the others. They may stumble, fall and try again, but everyone will appreciate their efforts. Small groups, cells and households are the best training ground for leadership development. Larger gatherings require greater levels of skill. If we expect to train leaders but the only gathering of the body is a large crowd gathering in an auditorium with a platform and significant distance between the leader and the audience, very few people will even be willing to try.

Much work and effort have gone into studying the effect of culture on leadership, including an excellent book by Jim Plueddemann, *Leading Across Cultures*.[8] Plueddemann evaluates the implications of various cultural patterns for leadership. One of these cultural patterns is known as "power-distance," identified in a massive research effort called the Globe Study, carried out in fifty-eight countries among midlevel managers. *Power-distance* is defined in the Globe Study as "the degree to which members of a collective expect power to be distributed equally."[9]

In a culture with high power-distance, the leaders are distant from the rest of the collective. They are respected, honored, even revered, and will often wear clothes that set them apart. They have more power, and the collective does not expect to share it. In a high power-distance culture, the pastor will have special training and special credentials and will be the only one allowed to officiate over certain rites of the church.

In a culture that has low power-distance, leaders have little more power than the people, and they are more likely to be considered as one of the group. Decision making is usually democratic in procedure. In a low power-distance culture, the pastor is more likely to share leadership with others, involving others as leaders in the various activities of the church.

I invited Antonio, Pablo and Sergio to form a pastoral team because I needed to find some way to keep the work going while I was gone, and no single person would be willing to assume responsibility. Without realizing it, I had introduced team leadership of nonordained disciples, a low power-distance solution to the issue of church leadership. Later, when we realized the long-term potential of a leadership team, the church decided to continue using that method.

Doing so, however, created serious contention with other Venezuelan pastors who had been trained to believe that the church should be led by one elder/pastor. The training they had received coincided with the natural tendency of Venezuelan culture toward high power-distance.

Whether power-distance is high or low, the end remains the same:

those in leadership have to find ways to empower and release the rest of the body into ministry. This may mean using countercultural solutions, and it certainly requires a great deal of humility.

As with the other slider switches, any ministry team will need to have a thorough discussion about these cultural dynamics and disclose how each person thinks. Once the issue is on the table for all to see, the team can begin to sort out which approaches are ones that will multiply gifting for the kingdom, instead of being designed for personal fulfillment.

Even though Western culture tends to be low power-distance, in a ministry setting missionaries can easily fall into high power-distance methods that make it difficult to train others in ministry. Doug, a good friend, taught a course on church planting at an evangelical seminary in the United States. On the first day of class he would ask each group of potential church planters, "Tell me your picture of success. If you achieve your dreams, what will it look like?" Gradually a picture emerged: the church planter in front of hundreds of people sitting in rows, listening with rapt attention. After some embarrassed laughter, Doug asked them to think deeply about the nature of the church and what they were really called to do.

Those from the West will identify readily with these potential church planters. Being the one whom people come to hear on Sunday morning produces a deadly delight. We like to be needed. We like the adulation. The notion of deriving value through hard work and competition creates identity for those from a Western background. But doing something well easily creates the trap that Roland Allen warns against. Subtly we become the one whom the new believers are following rather than Christ. We are making disciples, yes, but are they our disciples or disciples of Jesus Christ?

When this happens, the rest are not equipped to exercise their spiritual gifts for the building up of the body, or for carrying out the will of God in the world. An inverse relationship grows—the strong pastor often leaves a weak, dependent congregation. The slider switches are out of balance.

Extremely low power-distance can also have deleterious results on the health of the body. One movement in Venezuela grew because disciples were empowered to lead others as soon as they had received one Bible lesson from someone else. If disciple A shared the first Bible study with disciple B, then immediately disciple B was expected to share that study with disciple C, and so forth. The movement grew from a few hundred to almost six thousand in six years. The slider switch corresponding to disciples as ministers was set very high. Within a few more years, however, the entire movement began to disintegrate because the leaders did not have sufficient depth of understanding.

Strange, cultish practices began to grow within the movement. In a bizarre teaching, newly expectant mothers were given a stick with which to beat their bellies so that the fetus would learn discipline from an early age. After all, doesn't the Bible say that "whoever spares the rod hates their children" (Prov 13:24 NIV)? Clearly, this movement needed some well-grounded teachers who understood how to interpret Scripture. The slider switch of gifted and trained leadership was very low.

New cultural realities. Twentieth-century mission history, methods, models and marketing were carved out with full-time Christian workers locating in rural areas. The names of mission agencies from a century ago demonstrate this theme: Sudan *Interior* Mission, China *Inland* Mission, Africa *Inland* Mission. Missionaries went where the people were—inland. Because of the educational and economic disparity between the missionaries and those among whom they worked, missionaries often fell into the trap that Roland Allen so eloquently exposed. They instinctively started with high power-distance methods.

Enduring models of mission emerged, with equally famous images to promote them: for example, David Livingstone, wearing the now iconic pith helmet in the jungles of Africa, speaking to "natives" gathered under a banyan tree; or hospitals in distant rural areas curing diseases and sending home pictures of suppurating sores. Since rural people were often agrarian, a missionary in Africa or Latin America could spend many hours sipping tea, meeting people in front of their huts in the long afternoons, gathering tribal people together and telling stories or preaching.

Many of these men and women gave their lives in carrying the gospel to remote and hostile areas. In many ways, they are rightly considered heroes of the faith, and countless people worldwide have heard and accepted the good news because of them. Too often, however, they failed to train those to whom they ministered to use the gifts given by Jesus to the whole body, each depending on the Holy Spirit to carry out ministry within his or her own sphere of influence. Instead, a crippling dichotomy between clergy and laity too often emerged, leaving the vast majority of people sitting and waiting for someone to be trained just like the missionary in order to do ministry.

Fast forward to the twenty-first century; people are streaming into cities. Urban areas have schools, supermarkets, movie theaters, shopping centers, clubs, banks and employment. Time is at a premium. Instead of afternoons to chat with neighbors, the day is consumed with traveling through busy traffic to work, then struggling through the same traffic toward home. None of the old methods work.

Under these conditions, those who are gainfully employed are the front line of disciple making—well-equipped, empowered disciples— carrying the presence of Jesus into the workplace. To do that, leaders must empower and equip them.

Leaders lead best by equipping disciples to minister.

EXAMPLES OF LEADERS EQUIPPING MINISTERS

David Garrison's book *Church Planting Movements*[10] describes the astounding growth of the church in certain areas of the world today. These movements have both slider switches set in tension. Every disciple is trained to minister, exercising his or her own spiritual gifts. Qualified leadership is quickly recognized and empowered.

Finding the gift and unwrapping it. I loved it when anyone new walked into our small church for the first time. I began to think of each one as a gift, wrapped in bright paper, tied with a ribbon. My job as a leader was to untie the ribbon, take off the paper and see what gift the Lord had just brought into our church. In a previous chapter I told the story of Yelitza, who came to live with us for two years as she learned to follow Jesus. She was one such gift. As she began to grow, she wanted to do something. I had not yet realized that we needed to identify her base spiritual gifts, but the Lord had mercy on us.

I asked if she wanted to care for the small bookstore and lending library that we maintained. She willingly agreed, but within a few weeks we realized that math and accounting were not her strengths. After several weeks of trying to help her make sense of the records and bookkeeping, I asked if she wanted to be in charge of the coffee break that we had every Sunday after the message. Again she quickly agreed. But two weeks in a row she burned the coffee and had to serve juice instead. Then I heard that Child Evangelism Fellowship of Venezuela was holding teacher training classes, and I suggested that if Yelitza wanted to go to that, the church would pay the registration fee.

Through the CEF training, she discovered a gift of teaching that benefited the whole church. During the next several years she not only taught, but trained several others to teach as well. To watch someone grow, develop and become a leader, training and empowering still others, is an awesome experience.

Passing on leadership quickly. Salim was a member of a renowned Muslim terrorist group, connected to senior leaders. Because he was concerned for his personal salvation, he decided the only course that would guarantee his eternal destiny would be to become a suicide bomber. After training in handling explosives, he made preparations for his mission. He bid goodbye to his family, saying that he was going on a trip and would be back.

Then he had a dream: He saw his village in the distance, with all the villagers streaming out into the fields below him. Among them was a person head and shoulders taller than the rest, whom he recognized as Jesus. Jesus looked straight at him, walked through the crowd, came up to him and put his hand on Salim's forehead, saying, "Do not kill, do not lie, do not cheat." Then the vision vanished.

Salim was confused. He had just lied to his family and was setting out to kill as many as possible. Now the prophet Jesus had just told him not to do either. He began asking for advice from various religious leaders, describing his dream as one a friend had seen, but their only counsel was that he should have nothing to do with that friend. He dropped his plans for a suicide mission, slowly withdrew from active involvement in the terrorist group and became a teacher in a local school.

One day, while sharing his troubled thoughts with refugees from a neighboring country, one pulled a card from his pocket, saying, "These people have the answer for you." It was the address of a Bible correspondence school run by local Christians. He wrote to the school, and the first lesson he received in the mail was on the Ten Commandments. He was astonished to read, "You shall not kill." The Bible had given him the interpretation of his dream. He began studying the Bible avidly.

During this time, his wife developed extremely high blood pressure during a pregnancy, and they had to rush her to the nearest local hospital. The wife had a stroke and the baby died. Other believers told Salim about a mission hospital where his wife might get help. Deborah, a missionary physical therapist, helped his wife recover from the stroke over a period of a month of intensive rehabilitation. In the process the missionaries came to know Salim as a beginning follower of Jesus. As they helped him in his journey as a disciple of Jesus, they realized that he was a leader, and had family and friends throughout the area. They knew that their responsibility was to empower and equip him.

As Salim began sharing his faith with others, some came to faith in Jesus. Returning to Philip, one of the missionary doctors, he asked what they should do about baptism. Historically, the missionaries baptized new believers—functioning in a high power-distance mode. Now they realized that if every new believer had to be baptized by a missionary, it would impede the growth of the movement. With Salim and another leader, they studied closely what the Scripture said about baptism. Then Philip encouraged Salim and his colleague to baptize new believers in the way that would work for them. He would not even attend.

Salim and his fellow leader took the two new believers to a lake, found a spot for lunch on the lakeshore where no one was around, had communion together, then baptized them in the name of the Father, the Son and the Holy Spirit.

Handing over leadership to Salim demonstrated leadership training at its best, despite the sacrifice it involved on Philip's part. Salim was trained, empowered and released to function in his gifting as an apostolic leader. He continues to lead at great sacrifice and considerable personal danger.

The cutting edge of ministry is through the effective ministry of all disciples, with the leaders training, equipping, empowering and releasing them.

Training those who are already there. Filipino workers are streaming across the Middle East, finding employment in many places where professional missionaries are excluded. According to some estimates, eight million Filipinos are scattered throughout the Middle East and Asia. Approximately 10 percent of those are believers, already at work in some of the most difficult places on the planet. Church leaders from the Philippines are traveling to places where these people already have jobs, equipping them to be ministers of the gospel in the marketplace.[11] Filipina maids are carrying the gospel of the kingdom into the homes where they work, cleaning homes and caring for children.[12] They have their slider switches set in dynamic tension.

Disciples ministering where the people are. Missionaries who gain employment as residents in a given culture may have a more powerful witness than those who are in "Christian" institutions. In the Arabian Peninsula, one missionary nurse left the local mission hospital and taught as a nursing instructor in a nearby hospital run entirely by the government, normally hostile to Christians. Ironically, in the mission hospital, due to government pressure, she was under severe restrictions about what she could or could not do or say. But as an employee in the local hospital, she could have a much wider influence. She prayed regularly with the head of nursing and led Bible studies with other nurses, all in a hospital staffed and run by the local government of a Muslim nation.

A fellow mission leader began his missionary service as a medical researcher at a hospital in another country on the Arabian Peninsula. The people living there suffered from several genetic disorders because of the private and ingrown nature of that society. With the money they paid him for his research he was able to contribute enough to his mission agency to support two more missionaries. He had opportunities to demonstrate his competence as a medical researcher as well as his love for people in the name of Jesus. As an empowered disciple ministering in the marketplace, he enjoyed wide open doors for ministry. As a professional missionary, he would never even have been allowed to enter that country.

In this kind of employment setting, funding for ministry is a secondary benefit. Finding the means and mechanisms to enter the worlds in which people are living is the primary benefit. Just as missionaries entered the rural world of the last century, finding means and models that would allow the good news to enter their minds and hearts, we need to enter the urban world and explore the new avenues of global mission that are right before us.

Setting the slider switch in balance means that we can be full-time ministers of the gospel while being employed full-time as well.

Leaders Equip Disciples as Ministers

Leaders lead best by equipping others for ministry. Then the body, individually and as a community, can discern the will of God and carry it out, loving others and making disciples.

When leaders understand they cannot lead alone, but need leaders who comprise all five of the gifts listed in Ephesians, and when they understand that they succeed only when all of the disciples are equipped to minister and to become leaders themselves who can equip others, the impact and growth of the body is almost unlimited.

Disciples Live an Undivided Life

Public and Private

*And whatever you do, whether in word or deed,
do it all in the name of the Lord Jesus.*

COLOSSIANS 3:17 NIV

During a meeting of a small group of our suburban church, Jim, an accountant, said he was expected to deliver the budget for his company within a few days and requested prayer for wisdom. Thinking about the divide that often exists between the public sector and private faith, I asked whether anyone thought that God was interested in the budget itself, not just Jim meeting the budget deadline successfully. Greg, another member of the group, looked at me incredulously and said no. The inflection in his voice indicated how silly the question sounded to him.

I pushed the question further. Did God care about how well the business was run? Did God care about the welfare of all the people in that company whose lives the budget would affect? The thought slowly percolated through the group. All believed that God would hear prayer for Jim and his family, but like Greg, some members of the group struggled with the thought that God cared about everyone in the company, not just about Jim.

To be honest, the thought was fairly new to me as well. For many years, my faith and prayers circulated primarily within a private world of church, personal friends and colleagues. The rest of life—the neighborhood, local government, businesses, school system, environment or the economy—lay in the public sphere for which I was not responsible. I voted in elections, but did little else. I might have muttered and grumbled a bit about taxes and the public debt, but did not often consider those my spiritual responsibility or a matter for prayer.

Jesus is Lord of everything and everyone, not just of those people who call him Lord. Disciples live an undivided life, acknowledging Jesus as Lord of all.

My wife's stepfather cofounded what is today one of the largest family-owned food distribution companies in the United States. As a young man he married, had children and joined the Christian Business Association. One year, a tragic car accident took the lives of his wife and two of his three sons. As the Lord spoke to him in days of intense grief, he realized that he was called to serve God with his entire life, including all his business dealings. God redeemed the tragedy through his commitment to live for Jesus in church and business.

In his business, everyone began to realize that he would tell the truth, that he would honor God. Every year during the annual Christmas sales event, he would give a presentation of what Jesus meant to him, and how Jesus was the rock upon which the business was built. Eventually, he became the man to whom young men from his business or his church would go for counsel regarding their wives, jobs and finances. Occasionally they would complain, "But I don't make enough money to tithe." He would smile, graciously responding, "You don't make enough money *not* to tithe."

By the end of his life, he was giving away over a third of his income—so much that the IRS regularly booked him for audits because they could not believe that someone was giving away that much money. As a wise investor, he partitioned off some investments into a trust fund dedicated to charitable causes. Jokingly, over lunch one day, he told me how the trust fund kept multiplying and growing, while his other personal funds would gain and lose along with the stock market. My father-in-law had learned how to keep tension between the public slider switch and the private one. He was an astute businessman, and his company's solid growth was proof. He was completely dedicated to serving God through his business. He did not just see himself as someone who would earn money so that others could do the Lord's work; he went about the Lord's work daily as he made business decisions, managed employees and counseled those in need.

Dad Gordon lived an undivided life.

As a rule, Christians who live in the West have thoroughly accepted the public and private dichotomy. The public space, including government, education, business, law and communication, has become increasingly secular where spirituality and morality have little or no place. Morality and personal faith decisions occur in the private, individual space. Individuals flip back and forth between the public world and the private world, working in the public or secular sphere and moving into a private sphere on the weekends. A few hours of private time may be devoted to sacred activities.

The separation of church and state, instituted by the founders of the United States, did not preclude individuals in government from trusting and following God in terms of morality or ethics. Dollar bills in the United States proclaim "In God we trust." Today, however, the drift toward separation between the public and secular world and private or sacred worlds is almost complete, often leaving the public place morally bankrupt.

The slider switches of public and private are not in tension.

Other cultures don't recognize the need for both spheres. They align religion with the public space and depreciate anything else, including private faith. Some Muslim nations do not accept any division between public and private life, and religious law, or shari'a, governs all of life. The atrocities occurring in the "Islamic state" that emerged in 2014 in northern Iraq compare to equal horrors that occurred during four hundred years of the Inquisition.

Living at the extremes rather than living in tension at the center, leaves Jesus out of great sections of life.

MAINTAINING BIBLICAL TENSION: PUBLIC AND PRIVATE

Jesus lived without public and private boundaries. He did not compartmentalize. The Father governed every aspect of his life and work. Just before Jesus died he made the remarkable statement, "The world may learn that I . . . do exactly what my Father has commanded me" (Jn 14:31 NIV). Later, he repeats, "I have brought you glory on earth by finishing the work you gave me to do" (Jn 17:4 NIV).

Jesus was known in his hometown as the carpenter's son who had four brothers, James, Joseph, Simon and Judas, and at least three sisters.[1] Apparently Joseph, their father, had died and Jesus, as the eldest son, had been responsible for the family until he began his itinerant ministry. Whether he was quietly working as the carpenter's son or as the itinerant rabbi, he was doing exactly what the Father had commanded him. He entered into human life in every way, living and working with his fellow villagers. When the Father told him to go and be baptized, he left home and started on the three-year journey to the cross.

Jesus' every step was directed by the Father, whether staying in Nazareth for thirty years, traveling and praying with his disciples, turning over tables in the temple or confronting Pilate in his judgment hall. Jesus lived all of his life on that journey of obedience. What an aspiration—to say that we have done exactly what the Father has commanded us, in whatever sphere of influence or work we have been given. Obedience to the Father's will is the perfect guide through every situation of life, merging the public and the private.

The Pharisees thought they could trap Jesus with their question, "Is it right to pay the imperial tax to Caesar or not?" (Mt 22:17 NIV). They knew that he would get in trouble with the Herodians[2] if he said no, and with the Pharisees[3] if he said yes. He walked right through the trap by saying that one should recognize Caesar's earthly authority as well as God's ultimate authority: "Give back to Caesar what is Caesar's, and to God what is God's" (Mt 22:21 NIV). Jesus knew that Caesar served at his Father's pleasure, and that living by the tax guidelines of the time was another way of serving the Father. The public and the private, in dynamic tension.

In Ephesians, Paul uses the same argument to indicate how slaves and masters ought to treat one another.[4] Christ's authority could redeem even the reprehensible institution of slavery. Recognizing the absolute authority of Christ over both the slave and the master reduced both to equals. The best way for a slave to resist the dehumanizing power of slavery was to recognize that the master was not actually the master, but was himself a slave. Slaves could actually serve Christ through obedience to the master, and the masters were to treat the slaves as if they would receive the same treatment from their master, Christ himself. Paul did not recognize any boundaries between a public world and a private one. All of life was ruled by the principle of obedience to Christ, which was consequently obedience to the Father.

God does not care only about sacred activities. God hears the cries of everyone who is oppressed; he cares about all who are hungry; he yearns to help those who are depressed, blind or in prison. He loves foreigners and supports fatherless kids and their single moms.[5] Psalm 146 does not say that he loves only the foreigners, depressed or fatherless who are members of a church, or who have professed faith in him. He loves them all.

In the same way that word and works can be held in tension by asking the question, "How do I truly love my neighbor?" so also the public and private slider switches can be held in tension by asking the question, "What is my obedience to Christ?"

RECALIBRATING CULTURAL CATEGORIES

Ministry team members will have different cultural perspectives on these questions. Working through this set of slider switches is therefore critically important. Does God rule over all creation—public and private? Does he take pleasure in all that he has made—public and private? Does he rule only over those activities that we call private or sacred? Does he take pleasure in only what his children do and say?

One of the universal aspects of worldview, described by Kearney,[6] is categorization. A baby processes thousands, if not millions, of bits of data about the world. Since it is impossible to think about every piece of data separately, the child learns to categorize. From these earliest experiences, people develop assumptions about the best ways to organize the world around them.

Hiebert has given us a useful matrix to understand the variety of ways in which cultures categorize life.[7]

	Well-formed Sets	Fuzzy Sets
Intrinsic Sets	*Bounded*	*Intrinsic Fuzzy*
Extrinsic Sets	*Centered*	*Extrinsic Fuzzy*

Figure 8.1. Well-formed sets vs. fuzzy sets

Intrinsic sets are formed on the basis of the *essential nature of the members themselves....*

Extrinsic, or relational, sets are formed on their relationship to other things or to a reference point....

Well-formed sets have a sharp boundary. Things either belong to the set or they do not....

Fuzzy sets have no sharp boundaries. Categories flow into one another.[8]

Hiebert's book is well worth studying thoroughly, but for the purposes of this chapter we will only expand on two of the combinations above.

Bounded set cultures define things by internal or intrinsic characteristics. They make clear distinctions between that which is "in" and that which is "out." An apple is an apple because of its internal characteristics. An apple cannot be an orange.

Bounded set thinking is dichotomist in nature. Those who have been influenced by bounded set thinking are likely to create very clear lines between the public and private spheres of life and between the sacred and the secular, making it difficult to live a truly undivided life.

Missionaries from a bounded set culture will be eager to decide who has made a decision for Christ and who has not. Have they stepped over the line (boundary) and prayed a prayer of salvation? Are they members of the church or not? Have they been baptized? Have they taken the discipleship course or not? Once a new believer has crossed these lines, they are "in." But once in, now what? Continued growth and development, increasing understanding and intimacy with one another and with Christ present a challenge.

In bounded set thinking, life divides into the Sunday go-to-church person, the Saturday family person and the Monday through Friday businessperson, with little to no overlap. Certain behavior and dress may be expected when entering each space or time. Sacred activities occur within certain time and space boundaries; everything else is considered secular.

Those from this kind of a background will struggle with living an undivided life in which there is little or no distinction between public and private life.

Centered set cultures make a distinction between that which is "in" and that which is "out," but whether something is in or out depends on its relationship to the whole. Definers such as "ripe," "tall" or "old" are only clearly understood by their relation to something else.

Those from a centered set culture will be eager to develop relationships with others in the group and with the leader. They will want to increase in understanding and intimacy with one another and with Christ. When they arrive at the worship gatherings of the believers, they will interact with those whom they know, catching up on their relationship. For them, an increasing buzz of conversation before the more formal part of worship would be a sign of health, rather than total quiet.

One of the challenges for those from a centered set culture is to remember that the leader is Jesus, rather than those who lead the gatherings of the church. And since relationships are so important, any breakdown between people can wreak havoc with the whole group. Gossip can almost be worse than murder in these settings. Trust, once broken, may take years to restore.

Those from a centered set culture will have less difficulty in living an undivided life, with Jesus ruling over everything, but the variability of relationships makes commitment to a particular group much more fluid.

History has given us many examples of people who lived an undivided life, in public and private, the secular and the sacred.

A contemporary of C. S. Lewis, Dorothy L. Sayers was a Christian and a prolific author. In her day, a woman could not hold a teaching post in a major university, but since she was an intellectual, she needed to make her living somehow. During work in an advertising agency, she wrote a series of mystery novels whose protagonist was Lord Peter Wimsey. The series was immensely popular, and she eventually made enough money to study and write as she chose. Lord Peter was not a Christian, and throughout the series he never became one.

Some Christians criticized Sayers because they thought that surely she should cause her character to become converted. Sayers retorted that given his character, Lord Peter never would become a Christian. In order to tell the truth about life, she refused to bend the character so that people could consider the books "Christian" literature. The books are great literature in the genre, written by a Christian surely, but she refused to force Wimsey into the sacred space so that other Christians would be satisfied. She went on to write powerful books on how Christians ought to live, such as the classic, *The Mind of the Maker*.[9]

Alexandre Dumas's book *The Count of Monte Cristo* is not the dark tale of vengeance as sometimes portrayed, but rather reflections of Christological themes of justice and redemption. The three conspirators are, in the end, judged when truth prevails. Even in France during the tumultuous Napoleonic era, Dumas considered that all of life takes place under the watchful eye of God.

J. S. Bach's sacred music extends beyond church buildings. Whether one is reveling in the lush harmonies of *Come, Sweet Death,* or the glory of the *Mass in B Minor*, one's soul can't help but be lifted toward the divine.

In the book *Les Miserables*, Victor Hugo demonstrates what a bishop would look like if he lived like Jesus lived. The entire first section of the book describes the life of the bishop, who lives in every respect like he imagines Jesus would live in French society of the day. He is constantly living a life of obedience to Jesus in every detail. When Jean Valjean knocks on the door late at night, the bishop simply does what Jesus wants him to do. Starting from the other side of the public and private divide, he enters into the world asking the same question, "What is my obedience to Jesus in this situation?"

Sayers, Dumas, Bach and Hugo lived in a world far less divided between the public and private, sacred and secular.

As the director of TEAM, I was often invited to speak at mission conferences in various churches. One weekend I arrived early at a church in the Midwest and had time to get to know the pastor. He explained the various weekend activities, and then we began to explore our own backgrounds. He had formerly been the youth pastor and was now the senior pastor. He said that he had a rewarding time leading the youth ministry until a "Christian" school opened nearby. When that happened, the Christians pulled their children out of the nearby public school and sent them to the Christian school.

I still remember the sadness in his voice when he said, "They took my mission field away from me." Instead of Christian teachers, students and families being involved in the activities of their community and school, they had now developed a safe "Christian" enclave and had abandoned the world around them. Mission has not escaped this dichotomy. Similar sacred bastions called churches can easily isolate people from the communities around them.

EXAMPLES OF LIVING AN UNDIVIDED LIFE

Getting a job—particularly if you are a missionary in an urban area. My wife and I recruited a large team to go with us to Caracas, Venezuela, a city of five million people densely packed into a valley barely fifteen miles long. We were all trained in some form of ministry: Bible teachers, worship team musicians, preachers and evangelists. After the initial flurry of work involving language, cultural orientation and housing arrangements, we settled into the work of church planting. Then, to our dismay, we discovered how hard it was to find anyone interested in joining a Bible study, or in coming to our well-designed programs. We tried every outreach strategy we knew, then invented a few more. What was happening?

In Caracas, just about everyone had to work long hours each working day. One friend told me if he left for work at 6:15 a.m., it would take him a half hour to drive the five miles to work. If he left at 6:30, it would take him forty-five minutes, and if he left at 6:45, it would take him an hour. That meant he left for work at 6:15, and usually did not get home until evening. He would describe himself as *vuelto leña*, "good for nothing but firewood." He repeated the same routine every weekday. On Saturday morning he wanted to run errands, care for his car and do the things he did not have time to do during the week. Sunday morning he wanted to sleep in. Having a Bible study after twelve hours of work on a week night might be possible for the very highly motivated, but not otherwise. For the typical working person in the city, Sunday afternoon was the only discretionary time in which to explore something new or different.

Our team members had endless energy and were dedicated to making disciples, but unless we could get invited into a home on Sunday afternoon we had few opportunities to interact with people.

I once asked a Venezuelan, "How do you make new friends?" He looked at me incredulously and said, "You don't *make* friends." I said, "But if you go to a new place where you don't know anyone and you don't have any friends, what will you do?" He replied, "You take time to be with people, and friends *happen.*" Where could we have enough time to be with people for friends to "happen"? The obvious answer was the workplace. Patty had taken a job teaching English in a company that wanted all of their midlevel employees to learn English. She began to develop relationships, and to see some people beginning to follow Jesus as disciples. She had successfully navigated across the barrier between the secular and the sacred and was working as a Christian in the marketplace.

One day I saw an announcement in the local paper inviting musicians to try out for the Opera Choir of Caracas. They were going to produce the first Wagnerian opera since World War II, but the music called for a very large orchestra and choir, so they had to hire thirty additional voices. Kris and I applied, auditioned and were hired. For the next three months we invested three hours a night, five days a week, rehearsing *Lohengrin,* plus extra time to memorize the parts in German. During those three months, we had more interesting conversations about who we were and what we believed than we had had in three years previously. Everyone accepted us because we were competent musicians. That opened up the door to conversations and invitations into homes we might never have had otherwise. The barrier between the public and private vanished—we were Christians, disciples of Jesus, mixing it up with other musicians.

Unfortunately, the story did not end well. After the performances, which the President of Venezuela attended, some friends we made in the chorus invited us to their home on Sunday for a meal and to watch a video of *Lohengrin*. At that time our small groups of believers were meeting on Sunday evenings, so I calculated that we would have five hours to be with our new friends and I could still make it back to lead the small group for which I was responsible. But I miscalculated badly. The lunch took over three hours, and then they were going to watch the video, which was four hours long. Because of my commitment to leading the small group, we gave our apologies and told the hostess we had to leave. I remember saying, "I'm so sorry we have to leave. This is unforgiveable." She responded, "Yes, it is." That was the last we saw them.

How I wish I could go back and do that again. Our fellow church members would all have understood. We should have stayed, talked, interacted and only left when it was clear that everyone was going to leave. Unfortunately, I was acting in a bounded set culture of expectations, rather than a relational, centered set way. My duties in the sacred arena had interfered with a promising relationship. I lost the tension between the slider switches.

Loving your neighbor, whatever it takes. During the last two centuries, medical practitioners have led the way, pulling together the secular and the sacred. Hospitals and clinics throughout the world have combined the best medical care with love, compassion and a heart to tell people about Jesus. Some have quipped, "Which would you rather have—a good Christian, or a good doctor?" Wrong question. The question assumes a dichotomy between the public and private. What the world needs are good doctors who are good Christians at the same time. Thankfully, I have seen many who are world-class doctors and kingdom-class disciples of Jesus.

In October of 2005, approximately 100,000 people died and 125,000 suffered injuries when a massive earthquake shook the Himalayan mountains in Pakistan. Because of low construction standards, all the government hospitals in the area were either destroyed or so badly damaged that they were useless. Only one hospital was able to spring into action—a hospital built and run by disciples of Jesus. The buildings had been built according to the best construction standards, and the medical workers were among the best in the world. The hospital became the staging point for relief efforts throughout the hardest hit areas. Hospital workers prayed with the wounded, cared for their physical needs and listened carefully to their stories. They realized that although they could put splints on broken bones or give antibiotics for wounds, what people needed most was to have someone listen to them with love and concern as they poured out their grief. Within that environment, created by those who had no boundaries between secular and sacred work, Jesus walked among the patients. Thousands heard of Jesus for the first time. Through this hospital, since its humble beginnings in 1956, hundreds of thousands of people have heard of Jesus' love for them through the competent medical work and caring witness to the presence of Jesus.

Connecting with those involved in education. While we were in Caracas, we sent our children to an international school for three years. The normally exorbitant rates had fallen due to devaluation of the local currency. During those three years I discovered that the parent and family turnover rate was about a third every year. Within two years, I received an invitation to sit on a school board subcommittee.

More and more missionaries were moving into Caracas in those days, and most of them had small children. Soon the question of schooling came up. The instinctive response was to begin a "Christian" school. I wondered if we might make arrangements with the international school to provide teachers. Accordingly, I set up an appointment to speak with the principal. The principal said that they would prefer to hire resident certified teachers, rather than recruiting teachers at the international fairs who would only stay for two to three years—if we could provide them. She suggested that we could pool the salary and housing package of each teacher, using it to subsidize the cost of other missionary children.

At the next monthly meeting of missionaries who were working in the city, I explained the plan. They quickly objected. Someone had heard that they taught jazz and rock in the music program. Someone else had heard that they asked the children to meditate for a few minutes during the physical education activities. In short, it was not "Christian" education. We lost an amazing opportunity to develop relationships with hundreds of people in the middle and upper classes of Caracas. Instead, the missionary community created a small, struggling school with poor facilities, because we did not want any tension between our sacred and secular categories.

Over 1,800 international schools are functioning around the world. These schools attract the upwardly mobile of every country. Ministry teams of teachers could make daily contact with the global power brokers, and be paid to do it, if we could only remove the barrier between the secular and the sacred in our minds.

Doing business well. Business as mission is a growing phenomenon today, one which has challenged the dichotomy between the public and private. Steve Rundle and Tom Steffen have written an excellent book, *Great Commission Companies.*[10] While I was the director of TEAM, I once toured such a company in China. The business was a solid enterprise creating goods that were being marketed through outlets such as Home Depot and Lowe's. When I visited, they were experimenting with an entirely new product line because demand was falling in the United States for the previous product.

Amid all this activity, workers knew they would be treated fairly.

The owner found ways to employ disabled people. The employees also knew that they could join others in Bible study if they desired, although the owner was careful to avoid giving any impression that their jobs depended on their response to the invitation to join a Bible study or worship gathering. Many began to attend. In addition to working in a profitable business, many employees became disciples of Jesus.

The evangelical world has embraced business as mission because of the difficulty of getting religious worker visas to many places in the world, such as China or India. The truth is, we should be engaging in this kind of practice around the globe, even if getting visas for religious workers is possible. We live in an urban world and, if we are going to share Jesus with people, we have to be where they are—in the marketplace. In order to do this, though, we have to readjust our slider switch settings.

Creating a middle way. A pastor picked up the paper in Dublin, Ireland, one morning.[11] Two young women had taken their own lives the day before. One died in the doorway of a Catholic church. The other died on the street, smashed from drugs and alcohol. Something in the story implied that the legalism of the Catholic Church had probably driven the first to take her life—she probably felt she could not measure up. The other had gone the other way, trying to find meaning in drugs, alcohol and sex. As he sat, grieving for these lost lives, he thought there must be another way. Not religion. Not the world. But real disciples of Jesus getting close to lost young people like these two women.

He began to share his thoughts with other pastors and leaders in Ireland, including TEAM colleague Linda. Linda, a counselor by profession, was part of a church in the town of Swords, north of Dublin. The Lord gave their church an unusual opportunity to be involved in the local community, loving their neighbors.

One member of their church had some marshy property that they offered to donate to the church. Even though it was difficult to build on the property, he thought the church could use it for an investment. The property was valued at $140,000 at the time. In the ensuing years, the Irish economy, known as the Celtic Tiger, began to roar. In a few short years, the property sold for $5 million.

With this windfall in hand, they set out to invest in their local community. Church members often volunteer to help in any community activities planned by the local leaders. When the community leaders wanted to build a community center, the church donated a million Euros. Then, with the remaining cash, the church leaders proceeded to erect an auditorium for worship near the proposed community center, offering it for use by the community for meetings. When they opened the new auditorium, they invited a well-known community leader to be the master of ceremonies. The public and private slider switches were balanced in wonderful tension as the church's resources linked with community needs.

Disciples Live an Undivided Life

In an integrated, undivided life, Christians can serve God well through any honorable calling. Jim's work preparing a budget can bring God as much glory as singing on the worship team on Sunday morning. Watching *Lohengrin* with other musicians can be an act of obedience as meaningful as leading a Bible study.

Disciples who live an undivided life can connect with one another in the workplace, forming an interdependent community of disciples. They have the capacity to discern God's will together, to carry it out in their sphere of influence and to make disciples in the process. As they do so, their lives will change and so will the culture around them.

Disciples Engage in Personal and Cultural Transformation

Personal and Cultural

*Speak truth each one of you with his neighbor,
for we are members of one another.*

Ephesians 4:25

Culture is not benign. Every culture on earth, small or large, has within it that which reflects the image of God and that which reflects the fallen nature of the human race. With God's help and the wisdom of the Holy Spirit, disciples can identify personal and cultural patterns that reflect the kingdom of Christ, preserving, encouraging and developing those patterns. They must also identify evil patterns which are contrary to the kingdom of Christ, resisting those with all of their strength and developing countercultural approaches.

Disciples must contextualize the gospel where appropriate and act counterculturally when necessary. To do this, they have to start at the beginning—individual personal transformation with humility in the power of the Spirit of God. Once the journey has begun, it becomes possible to evaluate the groups to which they belong and which they can influence, such as one's own household, neighbors, friends, workplace, ministry team, small group, church, school or even larger groups as God provides opportunity.

As each larger group gets involved in the process, cultural transformation increases. When a church adds members from other cultures, their potential to bring about cultural transformation multiplies, and when churches work together, they can actually change the face of society. One day, when Jesus inaugurates his visible reign over all the earth, his disciples from every culture who have been purchased by his blood will "be a kingdom and priests to serve our God, and they will reign on the earth" (Rev 5:10 NIV).

Only when we have thoroughly evaluated our own cultural patterns, however, do we have any credibility in evaluating other cultures. This book provides a road map for some of those cultural questions and discussions.

Join me on a short journey of personal and cultural transformation:

Three of us bundled into the taxi to take us from the hotel to the airport. We were due to fly out of Xiamen, China, that morning, switch flights in Hong Kong, then fly on to Bangkok that afternoon. In Bangkok, we were to meet a chartered bus to take us to a hotel for a consultation of TEAM leaders. Two or three leaders were coming from each of thirty-five countries. As the international director, I felt a serious responsibility to arrive on time.

As the driver fought traffic on the way to the airport, I glanced at my tickets. To my shock, I realized that our layover in Hong Kong, one of the largest airports in the world, was only forty-five minutes. To compound matters, we had to change airlines from Dragon Air to Cathay Pacific, which meant that the departure gate might be in a different part of the terminal altogether. Immediately, I experienced a surge of adrenaline. A flood of worry swept over my mind and soul. Providentially, in preparation for the consultation I had just read a book, *Respectable Sins,* by Jerry Bridges.[1]

Bridges lists forty garden-variety sins that commonly occur among those who consider themselves disciples of Jesus, particularly in the evangelical tradition. Some sins are deadly and not at all respectable. "Respectable" sins are much more subtle, such as worry, selfishness, anger, judgmentalism, pride of correct doctrine, or godlessness. The author encourages the reader to make a list of all of the so-called respectable sins and rate each one: never a problem; sometimes a problem; often a problem; typical of me.

On my list, I had identified worry as one of the respectable sins that was often true of me. I have confessed it more than once. Now I was faced with a serious temptation to worry. After exclaiming to my traveling companions about our tight schedule, I stated, "Well, worry is a sin, so I'm going to trust the Lord with this one. That's my story, and I'm sticking to it." Everyone laughed.

When we boarded the plane, the stakes went up. We were seated in the last row, which meant it could easily take twenty minutes to disembark after landing in Hong Kong. When the flight was delayed twenty minutes, I kept repeating to myself, "I'm trusting the Lord on this. Regardless of what happens, he will look after us." We arrived in Hong Kong, taxied to the gate, and by the time we emerged from the door of the plane we only had fifteen minutes until our Bangkok flight was due to leave.

We saw a knot of passengers asking for help, gathered around an airline official with a clipboard. If we waited for her, we would lose the remaining fifteen minutes. Then I noticed a man dressed in a black uniform, standing alone a little way off. We went up to him, showed him our tickets and asked if he could give us directions to the proper gate. Without a pause, he said, "Follow me," and began winding his way through a deserted security check, up an escalator, down a hallway and finally to our gate. We walked on the plane and they shut the door. Did we meet an angel? I don't know—it sure seemed like we did. But I do know that my personal journey of transformation by the power of the Holy Spirit had taken a small step forward. I am so glad that I had decided to trust the Lord and not worry.

Now imagine that I'm in a group of believers—a ministry team, leadership team, small group or house church. Let's assume that I had not read *Respectable Sins* and had not identified worry as one of my sins. Imagine, too, that several others in the group share the same tendency to worry. As time goes on, expressing our worries becomes a pattern of the group, embedding itself in our group culture. When someone joins who does not have a problem with worry, he or she hears other mature believers worrying, so gradually also begins to worry. The pattern gradually becomes a spiritual fissure in the culture of the group. The original members can move on, but that spiritual fissure continues long after the original members have left and others take their place.

These so-called respectable sins have the capacity to subtly grow into patterns within any group of people. They can embed themselves in adult Bible classes, churches, ministry teams, mission agencies, networks, denominations and local or national cultures. Socialization occurs—that most powerful type of education—as new people gradually absorb the cultural traits of any group they join. Generations come and go, and these patterns continue. The only way to change is to confess these sin patterns publicly, inviting the Holy Spirit to transform the whole group, not just personal, individual lives.

During the consultation in Thailand, we had the opportunity to prayerfully and personally evaluate ourselves against the list of forty respectable sins and to confess them to God in the presence of two to three others. Small groups knelt throughout the meeting hall, praying, confessing and weeping. Then, using the same list, each leader evaluated the group of missionaries for which he or she was responsible. Some represented ministry groups that had been working for multiple generations; other leaders represented ministry teams that had been working together for only a few years. Together we recorded the sinful patterns that collectively existed among us.

We put our sin patterns into a spreadsheet and organized them from the most prevalent to the least. Then we projected, on a huge screen, the top ten sinful patterns that were true of our global organizational culture. In many cases, these patterns had prevailed for generations. As we looked, our mouths dropped open. We were looking in a cultural mirror. We caught a glimpse of how God saw us. With this reminder in front of us, we confessed our sins publicly. Then we celebrated communion together. What an awesome experience! The powerful cleansing work of the Holy Spirit began, not just in hearts of individuals, but in the culture of the organization itself.

This good beginning was a wonderful thing but should not be confused with overcoming sinful patterns. The first time I confessed my personal sin of worry was not the last; worry did not immediately lose its grip. Rather, I became more and more aware of it and had to confess it over and over again, until it slowly began to lose its hold. The same is true of organizational culture. Once we confess our sins the first time as an organization, we will then see them over and over and will have to keep coming back to the cross for forgiveness until the organizational culture is renewed.

I've used a negative illustration to make a point, but it works the same way with positive characteristics. Personal virtue and godly values, when these are embedded in a collective culture, also cause effects that will last for generations. The fruit of the Holy Spirit grows and ripens in our lives: courtesy is contagious; patience breeds peace; goodness absorbs and stops evil; love replaces hate.

If the slider switch is set high on the personal side of life and low on the collective culture side, disciples fail to realize the profound and far-reaching effect of sin and transformation on the cultures of which they are a part. But if the slider switch corresponding to culture is high and the personal low, disciples might get involved in legal and political causes without the credibility of personal life transformation. Pastors and politicians may rise to power on moral issues and then just as quickly prove that their personal lives lack the transformation they espouse for the culture in which they serve.

The journey of transformation moves back and forth, maintaining the tension between the slider switches. When we have embarked on this journey for ourselves and within our own cultures, we then earn the right, with humility, to do the same in other cultures.

MAINTAINING BIBLICAL TENSION: PERSONAL AND CULTURAL TRANSFORMATION

God designed the body of Christ to be a cultural force for the kingdom. He did not design it to be an engine of political enterprise.

The body of Christ grew within the Roman Empire, transforming the culture from the inside out, despite repeated waves of violent persecution. When Constantine declared Christianity the official state religion, appropriating the church for political ends, the combined entity of church and state entered into a long period of decline. A thousand years later, Constantinople fell to the Ottoman Empire. The destruction was staggering.[2]

Many of Paul's letters, including Ephesians, were written while being unjustly held in a Roman prison. While on an innocent trip to Jerusalem, he was falsely accused, thrown in prison, whisked away in the night to Caesarea, held for another two years without trial, sent to Rome on a boat (with an incompetent captain) and from prison was still waiting for justice to be served. Surely he had the right to whine just a little. Why weren't the elders of the church in Jerusalem organizing some political resistance? Where were the petitions or demonstrations for his release? Where was international pressure for human rights? Surely someone knew someone who could pull levers. Where was the political pressure?

Instead, what does Paul say? "Sing and make music from your heart to the Lord, always giving thanks to God the Father for everything, in the name of our Lord Jesus Christ" (Eph 5:19-20 NIV).

Unbelievable. Countercultural.

Yet at the same time, he demonstrated appropriate contextualization by endorsing the authority structures that existed for the preservation of law and order within Roman culture and by using his Roman citizenship when necessary and proper to do so.

When Onesimus,[3] a runaway slave, experienced his own personal transformation, what did Paul do? He sent him back to his master, Philemon, who had also experienced a personal transformation. Instead of Philemon giving Onesimus a legally permissible death sentence, Paul pled with Philemon to accept Onesimus back as a brother. Paul did not organize marches on the Roman senate, asking for an end to slavery. Instead, he undermined it by energizing Philemon to live in a countercultural pattern.

Paul is well aware that some of the cultural patterns of the world around him were filled with evil.

And you were dead in your trespasses and sins, in which you [plural] formerly walked according to the course of this world, according to the prince of the power of the air, of the spirit that is now working in the sons of disobedience. Among them we too all formerly lived in the lusts of our flesh, indulging the desires of the flesh and of the mind, and were by nature children of wrath, even as the rest. (Eph 2:1-3)

In response to this decadent situation he instructs them how to live counterculturally. "Be angry, and yet do not sin; do not let the sun go down on your anger" (Eph 4:26). Become people that keep short accounts, rather than letting gossip, triangulation and bitterness gain a foothold.

"He who steals must steal no longer; but rather he must labor, performing with his own hands what is good, so that he will have something to share with one who has need" (Eph 4:28). Don't hoard your wealth. Give it away. Develop philanthropy, giving to those in need—trusting that God will continue to provide.

"Let no unwholesome word proceed from your mouth, but only such a word as is good for edification according to the need of the moment, so that it will give grace to those who hear" (Eph 4:29). Build others up rather than tearing them down.

These exhortations are countercultural in every society throughout history.

When these patterns grow in influence, good things happen. People feel safe, cared for and encouraged. Neighborhoods become places where people thrive. Children are not traumatized by fighting parents.

The most countercultural of all was Jesus himself. Consider his Sermon on the Mount.

"Blessed are you who are poor, for yours is the kingdom of God" (Lk 6:20 NIV). Really? This passage is difficult to understand for those in bounded set cultures because there is no clear delineation of how much or how little money it takes to qualify as being poor.

What Jesus meant was the same thought Paul echoed years later in his letter to the Ephesians: Learn to give away your money to those who have greater need than you do. Learn to trust God, even when giving hurts. Learn the art of being poor with peace. Move in the direction of poverty. When you do, you will be surprised. You will be blessed. If you become a channel for God's blessing, he will continue to bless you. The more you give, the more he will delight to let pass through your hands, an instrument of the kingdom.

And this is only the beginning. Consider "Blessed are you who hunger now" or "love your enemies" or "do good to those who hate you" (Lk 6:21, 27 NIV).

The body of Christ has a mandate to be a countercultural force in the world. Rather than glossing over these hard passages, disciples of

Jesus need to learn from them and apply them, to let kingdom values shine through.

NAVIGATING TRANSFORMATION IN GUILT AND SHAME CULTURES

Culture either contributes toward or diminishes the power of the body of Christ. By now, we should be acutely aware of some ways in which cultural settings have been reflected in a ministry team, small group, church or society; hopefully we should be ready to make some changes. But change is difficult, and cultural change is uncomfortable. Granted, there is much we do not understand about other cultures. But cultural humility is not the same as cultural relativism. Some things are right and some are wrong.

Engaging in personal and cultural transformation is a challenge everywhere: How much like the French (or Japanese or Russians) should I become in order to make disciples? When have I gone too far? When should the body of Christ become countercultural? These are the questions that constantly emerge as crosscultural workers wrestle with these two slider switches.

Missionaries are thinking deeply and seriously about cultural issues, working hard to determine the appropriate degree of adapting to the context, accepting some patterns and rejecting others. Workers among Muslim populations constantly debate the level of adaptation to the culture to which they will go as followers of Jesus Christ.

Guilt cultures and shame/honor cultures. To determine what is right and wrong, however, implies that we have some standards by which to judge, and once again culture itself influences those standards. Duane Elmer, in *Cross-Cultural Conflict*[4] and *Cross-Cultural Connections*,[5] has done an admirable job of summarizing the differences between cultures that emphasize guilt and restitution and those that emphasize shame and honor.

In a guilt-based culture, any wrong generally has to be traced to an individual, who is then expected to own up to it, ask forgiveness and give restitution. The individual who committed the wrong is guilty and expected to feel guilt. Anyone who commits wrong and does not feel guilt may be considered psychologically impaired. In the organizational culture of institutions, such as colleges, companies or schools, when wrong occurs someone "has to take the fall." When abuse occurred in the Penn State football program, the perpetrator, the coach and the university president all had to share the blame, assume the guilt and pay the price.

In shame-based cultures, anything that makes one's group or family look bad in the eyes of others is considered shameful, something to be avoided at all costs. These cultures are also considered "face" cultures. To have others think well of me and the group of people to whom I belong brings honor. If something I do causes others to speak badly about me or my family, I have brought shame on them and have lost face. However, if something I do causes others to speak well of me or my family, I have brought honor to them.

Individualist cultures tend to be guilt cultures, and collective cultures tend to be shame cultures. Both have strengths and weaknesses. Both are addressed in the Bible. David sings "my salvation and my honor depend on God" (Ps 62:7 NIV).

Personal and cultural transformation require understanding of the cultural and countercultural ways of identifying and correcting that which is wrong.

Taiwan is a shame/honor culture. A colleague, Judson, reported that the American group called Peacemaker Ministries gave a seminar to Taiwanese pastors on resolving conflict. At some point in the seminar, the American presenter gave an illustration of someone who came to the point of saying, "I was wrong. Please forgive me." The pastors objected, saying that it would be impossible for them to say such a thing, because they would lose face in front of their whole congregation, making it impossible to carry on ministry.

At the time, Judson was mentoring a young man, Chang, who wanted to become a pastor. Chang had offended an older woman in his congregation, and the relationship was strained. Judson and Chang discussed Bible passages about forgiveness and restitution. Chang agreed that to admit sin and ask forgiveness was the right thing to do, but found it impossible, because he would lose face. Finally, after six months, he reported that he had met with the woman and admitted his sin, asking for forgiveness. To his surprise, instead of losing face with her, her respect for him grew and their relationship was restored. The event precipitated a small revival in the church. Chang had taken a countercultural approach, prompted by Judson and by the Holy Spirit.

In an African country, we suffered a complete breakdown in the relationship between our organization and African church leaders. The leaders wanted ownership of property that belonged to the mission agency, and the ensuing debate became contentious. Eventually the leaders prohibited missionaries from stepping over the thresholds of their church buildings. Efforts by the missionaries to resolve the issue only made things worse.

About ten years later, the church leaders began an informal discussion with mission leaders. They began talking about things of mutual interest, carefully leaving the former issue out of the discussion. Gradually, a working relationship was restored, culminating in a feast celebrating their reconciliation. The relationship had been restored in a way that did not shame either party. One of the church leaders reported, "During the last ten years we have seen that right or wrong cannot be determined by the color of one's skin. We need each other." In this case, complete reconciliation occurred in a culturally appropriate way.

Which sin is worse? Not only do cultures differ in how to reconcile with one another after a conflict, they also differ in what sins are better or worse than others. In Venezuela, to avoid greeting or bidding goodbye to someone when entering or leaving a group can bring shame and cause serious offense. On the other hand, sexual relations are generally considered a biological function without moral value, and are allowed as long as no shame is brought on the family. A wife may say, "You are my husband as long as you are in my house." The husband, "You are the cathedral, but there are lots of churches."[6]

In other cultures, such as Pakistan, getting angry at someone in public may be one of the worst possible sins, bringing shame on that person, his family and neighbors. Other sins, such as lying, may be considered appropriate when doing so saves the collective from shame.

In the United States, not being politically correct is considered one of the worst cultural sins, while anger is dismissed as a passing emotion. Consumerism, on the other hand, is culturally appropriate, as is "Sportianity . . . a mix of locker-room psychology and athletically slanted doctrines of assertiveness and masculinity, abetted by cherry-picked Bible verses prescreened to ensure they don't contradict sport's reigning orthodoxies."[7]

The sad fact that Sunday morning in the United States is largely a segregated time of the week is a testimony to our failure to be a countercultural force for the kingdom. The same is true of class. If everyone in the church is dressed well, with the latest hairstyles, shoes and accessories, how will someone feel who walks in with old, dirty or torn clothes? One church leader quoted a visitor as saying that he was not coming back because he simply could not dress as well as the rest.[8] Culture is most apparent to the outsider, and without strong efforts to transform our cultures as well as our personal lives, outsiders will feel left out or simply go away.

EXAMPLES OF PERSONAL AND CULTURAL TRANSFORMATION

Expanding and evaluating the list. The list of sins developed by Bridges could be useful in crosscultural situations. Starting with his list, a multicultural group could expand and include other types of sin patterns. Then each person who represents a different culture could explain which sins were considered most grievous, together with appropriate means of resolution.

Finding cultural clues to the kingdom. When missionaries began living among the tribal people of Papua, they encountered customs that glorified treachery, killing and eating one's neighbor.[9] Cultural relativism was impossible—surely these practices were wrong, no matter what anthropologists at the time were saying. Missionaries who entered the tribal societies in Papua saw firsthand the destructive results of disease, distrust and tribal warfare. These jungles were no pristine Garden of Eden. Far from it. Yes, the various tribes had characteristics that were delightful and reflected the glory of God, but evil was also present.

Don Richardson's book *Peace Child* tells the story of two tribes that demonstrated a cultural way of reconciliation by taking a child from one tribe and giving it to another to be raised by that tribe.[10] As long as the child was alive and well, peace would endure. Richardson realized that he could use their cultural custom to explain the good news in a way they could understand. When he did so, they understood that God had sent them a peace child in the person of Jesus, giving his own son to the human race. Collectively, they decided to follow Jesus. Richardson implied that every culture has patterns or myths that can be used to teach the truths of the kingdom of God.[11]

Fifty years later, Richardson and his three sons had an opportunity to return. They were amazed. For the first time in their history, people were living long enough to become old. Before the arrival of the gospel, many who could not fight vigorously were killed. Now the Richardsons met people living into their sixties and seventies. Three tribes that had been sworn enemies were now intermarrying, living together, working together, combining the nascent economies of all three groups and, most important, worshiping together.

Richardson and his sons were overcome at the cultural transformation that had been brought about by the good news of the kingdom of Jesus Christ.[12]

Keeping the dream alive. While living in Caracas, I became friends with the hardware store owner who lived across the street. One afternoon as we were chatting, he complained about rising rates of crime in the city. Often, such complaints were accompanied with nostalgic comments about how safe everything was under the last dictatorship.

I turned to him and said, "Can you imagine what this city would be like if everyone obeyed just one of the Ten Commandments? Just one, such as 'Don't steal'?" We began musing about the changes that would occur. No need for bars on all the windows or steel doors with triple locks or pins that rotated into the doorjambs and the floor. Cars could leave their windows open in the heat. We would not hear the ever-present wail of car alarms. We would not need as many police, lawyers or judges. The government would have enough money for all of the public services. Government contracts would be fulfilled. Street lights would stay on; fear would dissipate.

I knew that many Roman Catholics who lived in Venezuela regarded the Ten Commandments as highly restrictive—commands that sucked the fun out of life. But obeying just one of the Ten Commandments would almost turn the city of Caracas into a paradise. This was not bondage to legalism; this was freedom. I don't know if the thought stayed with that store owner, but it has stayed with me. When Jesus explained the story about the weeds and the wheat, he said, "The Son of Man will send out his angels, and they will weed out of his kingdom everything that causes sin and all who do evil. . . . Then the righteous will shine like the sun in the kingdom of their Father" (Mt 13:41-43 NIV). Paradise found.

Taking the good news to those who need it the most. In the heart of Chicagoland, a church is thriving in the neighborhood known as the Little Village, or in Spanish, *La Villita.* Most people in the community are Hispanic, and gangs rule the night.

One night a few years ago, shortly before Easter, a young child was killed in a drive-by shooting. The pastor got up the Sunday before Easter and challenged the men of his congregation. He told them to meet him at the church building at 10:00 p.m. on the Saturday before Easter and instructed each one to bring a bag of doughnuts. They were going to find and talk to the gang members. Realizing that some of the men would be afraid, he said, "Can you think of a better night to die than just before the day we celebrate the resurrection?"

About twenty men joined him. That night, they crossed the boundaries and talked to gang members and leaders. They brought peace, at least for one night, to these troubled youth. What a difference between that and more police protection. This is the power of the good news. This is countercultural.

Tearing down strongholds. Long and deeply embedded cultural patterns can become strongholds against the gospel. Living in the suburbs has been a challenge for us. Garage doors open and close. People go into their houses, only to drive away to work again the next day. Neighbors usually only see each other when they mow their lawns in summer or shovel snow in winter. People can live next door to each other for decades and not know each other. The pastor of a suburban church recently said that he believed a spirit of isolation had saturated the suburbs. The longer one lives in the suburbs the more isolated one becomes. Within a short while, a person who moves in begins to think it normal not to know the neighbor's name.

Churches generally try to overcome this isolation by inviting people to their church activities, getting to know people there, but this does nothing to overcome the isolation of living next to someone you do not know. Too often, the activities of the church only make it more difficult to meet one's neighbors by cutting into the little time that is available.

In *The Suburban Christian*, Al Hsu has given us some valuable suggestions for how to overcome this spirit of isolation, including simple hospitality, borrowing from one's neighbors or simply inviting a neighbor to run an errand together.[13] We have been praying that the Lord will overcome the spirit of isolation in our suburb, that he will allow us to mix it up with others, living life together, loving our neighbor as ourselves. Slowly we are beginning to overcome the cultural barriers. We have developed a neighborhood gathering once a month and, with help from neighbors, have had some successful block parties. A neighbor recently asked to borrow a tool. Another rang the bell and asked about getting rid of some unwanted construction debris. Gradually we are overcoming the isolation.

DISCIPLES ENGAGE IN PERSONAL AND CULTURAL TRANSFORMATION

"Getting saved" is not enough. "Going to church" is not enough. Under his leadership, Jesus calls us on a journey together of continual transformation, personally and culturally. When we follow him on this journey, we experience transformation as his disciples, and our capacity to make disciples of others increases. As we learn to judge our personal and our cultural values by the values of the kingdom, it gives meaning to our prayers: "Thy kingdom come."

Disciples Keep the End in Mind

Church and Kingdom

But seek His kingdom,
and these things will be added to you.

LUKE 12:31

Jesus, incarnated into human history, invited us to join his cause, the greatest cause in the history of the universe. One day men and women "from every tribe and language and people and nation" will be gathered around his throne, "a kingdom and priests to serve our God, and they will reign on the earth" (Rev 5:9-10 NIV). Corruption and crime eliminated. Greed gone. Death and disease overcome. Oppression eradicated. The perfect, loving, just King ruling in all his glory. That is good news! Amazingly, I can be a part, as long as I am willing to give up my own little kingdom.

In Tolkien's magisterial story *The Lord of the Rings*,[1] four hobbits set out from their home in the Shire on an errand to deliver a small gold ring to the wise elf Elrond who lives many days' travel away. What starts out as a lark with a group of friends quickly turns into a battle between good and evil. The hobbits endure cold, heat, thirst, hunger, hardship and danger as they flee from Black Riders. One night they are trapped in a confrontation on a hill named Weathertop. In the ensuing battle, the poisoned tip of an evil dagger breaks off in Frodo's shoulder and gradually works its way toward his heart. As they flee toward the safety of Elrond's house, the four hobbits realize that they are part of a much bigger story. At Elrond's house, Frodo gradually recovers his strength with the help of elf healers, while the hobbits rest, talk, sing songs, share stories, eat, drink, plan and celebrate.

Mark Buchanan, a pastor writing about the theme of rest and the Sabbath, says that their time at Elrond's house is a good picture of the church, on Sabbath together.[2]

After they have rested and recovered, the Council of Elrond, consisting of elves, dwarfs, men and hobbits, charges Frodo to destroy the ring in the fires of Mount Doom where it had been forged and commissions the Fellowship of the Ring, appointing members who represent all the races. Together, they set out into the dark kingdom of the evil Sauron, risking their lives to defeat him and to restore Middle Earth to its people, establishing the kingdom of light.

In contrast to the picture of the church on Sabbath at Elrond's house, this is a picture of the church on mission together.

What would have happened to Middle Earth if the Fellowship had decided to stay at Elrond's house? If they had refused to face the unknown dangers that lay in their path for the sake of the kingdom of free people? If they had chosen the comfort, security and safety of the Fellowship, rather than the bruising, life-threatening battles that lay ahead to keep Middle Earth from falling entirely under the sway of evil?

In this pair of slider switches, one corresponds to Sabbath activities, including corporate worship, eating together, teaching, sharing stories, praying together, fellowship and rest, which build up the body of Christ, preparing us for the work of the kingdom. The other switch corresponds to involvement of the church in the life of the community, city or nations—seeking the kingdom of Jesus Christ.

When we give equal priority to Sabbath activities *and* kingdom activities, then the two switches are set in dynamic tension.

However, if the slider switch representing Sabbath activities is set high, but the mission slider switch is set low, then neighbors, friends and even family who are not yet part of the church may feel ignored. Some, upon becoming believers, drift away from their old friends and within one to two years no longer have friends outside of their church circle, thus losing the ability to renew society and transform culture. The kingdom does not come.

If the kingdom activities switch is set high and the Sabbath activities switch set low, disciples may invest wholly in political, economic, social or kingdom causes, leaving behind any commitment to the body. Without the spiritual power of the body of Christ, these causes cannot provide the depth of solutions necessary. William Easterly, in *The White Man's Burden*, documents how the West has spent trillions of dollars in aid over several decades, but has virtually nothing to show for it.[3] Aid dollars cannot change the human heart. Aid dollars may, in fact, increase corruption because of the human heart. Only the body of Christ has the solution that can effect change within the human heart.

The work of the kingdom cannot succeed without the church, and the church fails if it does not engage in extending the kingdom. The commission given to Frodo to throw the ring into the fires of Mount Doom would have failed miserably had it not been for the entire Fellowship and the unique contribution of every member. While Frodo struggled up the hot, burning sides of Mount Doom, the rest of the Fellowship threw themselves toward the awful gates of Mordor to gain just a bit more time for Frodo to succeed.

During their time at Elrond's house the Fellowship worked together, planned and made preparations for their journey, sharpened their weapons and told stories. But they did not stay there. They set out on their mission into the unknown darkness. The church gathered is not the end of what we have been called to do, but the means to the end which is the kingdom of the King of kings, Jesus Christ.

Disciples keep the end in mind.

Maintaining Biblical Tension: Church and Kingdom

Many voices have called for better integration of the church and kingdom: *The Tangible Kingdom* by Hugh Halter and Matt Smay,[4] *Gods That Fail* by Vinoth Ramachandra,[5] *The Jesus Creed* by Scot McKnight[6] and *The Divine Conspiracy Continued: Fulfilling God's Kingdom on Earth* by Dallas Willard,[7] to name a few.

What is surprising in light of these works is how easily the notion of the kingdom becomes absent and how quickly churches focus only on the church gathered rather than on the kingdom.

A critical link between theology of the kingdom and theology of the church is the person of Jesus, who is both King of the kingdom and head of the body. Paul describes Jesus seated in the heavenly places. From that position, he has total authority over every person known in human history. All rule, authority, power and dominion are subject to him.[8] He is King of kings and Lord of lords.

Amazingly, we, the body of Christ, are seated with him, right now, in that position of power and authority. Furthermore, as King, he has been given to the "church, which is His body, the fullness of Him who fills all in all" (Eph 1:22-23). Jesus infuses the church with his presence, and the church fights for his honor, extends his kingdom and carries out his will. With his glorious return at the culmination of history, Jesus will be revealed as King.

Consequently, Paul gives very specific instructions telling believers how to carry the kingdom into their everyday lives. As a living illustration, Paul points out that as the King, Jesus rules over both husband and wife, giving to both the role model that will cause the marriage to thrive.

He also shows how his disciples should represent the King in society: "But immorality or any impurity or greed must not even be named among you, as is proper among saints; and there must be no filthiness and silly talk, or coarse jesting, which are not fitting, but rather giving of thanks" (Eph 5:3-4).

In this visible world we have a job to do for Jesus. That job may look small, insignificant or dangerous, because we usually have little idea what is at stake. Jesus knows what we should do, though, because he is the Alpha and the Omega. He sees the end from the beginning. He rules through those who have bowed the knee before him as King and have sworn allegiance and obedience to him.

A colleague of ours in Venezuela was approaching retirement when, for the first time in Venezuelan history, someone who represented the evangelical movement decided to run for president. Many Venezuelans we knew were ecstatic. They believed that through this person everything would be set right, because he was a fellow disciple of Jesus. Our colleague was appalled. He invested his final year before retirement in convincing as many people as possible that local churches and fellow believers should stay out of politics.

I now realize that both of these views were flawed. Even if the evangelical candidate were to be elected (which did not happen), he alone would not be able to set all things right, even from that position of power. He could, however, speak the truth, insist on justice and live in obedience to the King of kings.

On the other hand, our ministry colleague had a view of the kingdom that was so far out in the future, or so far beyond this world, that it had no correlation to the present. In his view, the church was to be engaged only in its own business, ignoring the wider world. Both our colleague and our Venezuelan friends were experiencing the tension that exists between the kingdom "already" here in the person of Jesus the King and the kingdom "not yet" here in all of its glory.

Jesus is the perfect King, and he has "already" come. More than that, he inaugurated his kingdom on earth and was raised to the highest position in the universe. Someday he will come in all his glory, but he is not waiting until then to invite us to share in his kingdom. All of life, every human endeavor, belongs to him as King. When the apostle John had a vision of his glory, he heard the angels singing the refrain, "Worthy is the Lamb, who was slain, to receive power and wealth and wisdom and strength and honor and glory and praise" (Rev 5:12 NIV). Humans invest time and effort in accumulating power, wealth, wisdom, strength, glory, honor and praise, but it all belongs to Jesus, it has all come from him and it is all going back to him. He owns it all.

Although the millennial kingdom has not yet come with Christ in his glory ruling and reigning, nonetheless, every person who serves Jesus as his disciple also vows to serve him as King: "Your kingdom come, your will be done" (Mt 6:10 NIV). We can rejoice when disciples of Jesus engage the world in politics, scholarship, arts and every other worthy endeavor.

Keith McCune, a missionary serving with TEAM, comments:

> The metaphor that kills this kind of engagement is the Titanic metaphor. If planet earth is the Titanic (so goes the metaphor), then the only activity that matters is packing the lifeboats. Why would you bother to improve the wallpaper? Or organize a waiters' union? Or improve the lodgings down in the steerage class? Or join the brass section of the orchestra?[9]

So why bother with saving Middle Earth? Why not just join the elves and go to the Grey Havens?

Titanic theology is an illustration of the slider switch corresponding to Sabbath activities set high and the switch corresponding to kingdom or mission activities set low. These settings lead to an imbalanced view in which the church is a safe lifeboat, rather than the view in Matthew

16 in which the church is crashing battering rams against the very gates of hell.

The *Titanic* view also contrasts sharply with Jesus' parable of the wheat and the weeds:

> As the weeds are pulled up and burned in the fire, so it will be at the end of the age. The Son of Man will send out his angels, and they will weed out *of his kingdom* everything that causes sin and all who do evil. They will throw them into the blazing furnace, where there will be weeping and gnashing of teeth. Then the righteous will shine like the sun *in the kingdom* of their Father. (Mt 13:40-43 NIV)

Everything about this broken world in which we live is already his kingdom, even if significant portions of it are in rebellion.

During the period of time following the Russian Revolution, E. Stanley Jones, a British missionary to India, visited Moscow. He was amazed at the will and discipline of the people working to build a new society. He saw thousands of people laboring by hand to build the Moscow underground subway system, singing songs of the revolution. In his book *The Unshakable Kingdom and the Unchanging Person*, he proclaimed,

> The greatest loss that has ever come to the Christian movement in its long course in history was this loss of the kingdom. For the thing that Jesus called the Good News, the Gospel, has been lost. Not silenced, but lost as the directive of the movement. . . . The substitutes became the goal. The Church became the kingdom, the Church with all its manufactured claims to infallibility. . . . A crippled Christianity went across the Western World, leaving a crippled result. A vacuum was created in the soul of Christendom, the kingdom of God became individual experience now and a collective experience in heaven. Between

that individual experience now and the collective experience hereafter in heaven vast areas of life were left out, unredeemed—the economic, the social, and the political. Into that vacuum the earthborn totalitarianisms moved.[10]

The "earthborn totalitarianisms" to which he referred led to countless deaths during and after the Second World War.

When both slider switches are set opposite one another in dynamic tension, a gutsy "already" kingdom theology results. Mission is the church storming the gates, with a common purpose to glorify the King. This can happen when members of the body of Christ serve the King in the domains into which they are called, such as the arts, politics, biochemistry, carpentry or any other career, counting on the spiritual power inherent in the body. Missionary ministry teams function as a mobile "dwelling of God in the spirit" with the capacity to bring the power of the almighty God into any situation (Eph 2:22).

Churches—Islands Within Culture or Force for the Kingdom?

During the centuries that preceded railroads, automobiles, airplanes, telephones and the Internet, people often lived in the same town or village all their lives. Work ebbed and flowed with the seasons. Relationships were the stuff of life. People knew people. Families knew families. Marriage and community provided stable roots for relationships to thrive. Of course, people would occasionally move away or travel to distant parts, but they would usually come back. I caught a glimpse of this kind of world while doing research in Venezuela. In small towns, everyone knew everyone else. They might not have known the first name of everyone, but they knew the last name, and they knew where those people lived.

The book *Anne of Green Gables*[11] paints an attractive picture of this kind of society. People knew their neighbors, they worked in the same town, shopped in the same grocery store and attended school events with the same people. They nursed one another's children and rejoiced in one another's victories. School, work, neighborhood and the marketplace combined and overlapped. On Sundays, they gathered for worship. They were a community of interrelated people who gathered for worship in their common faith.

Wherever mobility, secularism, urbanization and individualism increased, these various circles began to separate.[12] Today, people rarely live in the same neighborhoods as the people with whom they work. They rarely shop in the same stores as their neighbors. Schools used to be one place that an individual could count on meeting a neighbor; that, too, is shifting. During this process, the church became identified more and more with the building in which the community worshiped and gradually drifted away from identity with the community. The church became an isolated place of worship and teaching, rather than an integrated part of the community and a force for good within the culture. The kingdom impact of the people of God diminished accordingly. Paul Sparks, Tim Soerens and Dwight J. Friesen have written extensively about this dilemma in *The New Parish*.[13]

While doing research in Venezuela for a postgraduate degree, I interviewed evangelicals and nonevangelicals alike on the theme of Venezuelan worldview. One of my questions sparked a sharp retort: "Why do evangelicals do so little for the community? The Catholic church has all kinds of programs, but the evangelicals seem content with going to church." Ouch. He knew I was an evangelical, and he knew that I helped to teach Bible studies and start churches. His mother had even been involved in one of our Bible studies.

He had revealed my default settings. I had invested most of my time and attention in building up groups of disciples into a local church, teaching them how to study the Bible and feed themselves spiritually, how to worship, how to pray. I had assumed that the impact of these church activities would automatically seep into the surrounding community through (hopefully) transformed lives of the individuals. I had invested in Sabbath activities but failed to help them see the implications for the kingdom.

Recently I heard an African bishop in the Anglican communion express the same default setting, saying, "Our job is to bring as many people into the church as possible, and then shepherd them on into heaven."[14] The direction of his leadership efforts was to extract as many people as possible out of the world. If this were the case for the *Fellowship of the Ring*, their task would have been to convince as many people as possible to flee to Elrond's house to wait for the journey to the Grey Havens, letting Middle Earth slide into darkness.

Historically, however, global mission has been at the forefront of kingdom causes in poor and struggling countries, creating hospitals and schools, promoting literacy and engaging in community development. Rural communities around the world desperately needed and welcomed these services. These causes may have been simply the means to the end of getting churches started, not necessarily the other way around. Instead of making disciples who gathered, prayed and planned how to bring the kingdom to their part of the world, the view of the Anglican bishop often prevailed. Their intent, as mine, was to get as many people as possible out of the world and into the "lifeboats" of the church.

More recently, particularly in resistant areas, ministry teams have engaged in for-profit enterprises through business as mission. Sometimes they have done so because they view their business as an opportunity to transform society and redeem culture as an expression of the kingdom, increasing the number of disciples in the process. But sometimes they view their business enterprise as mere scaffolding, to be dismantled once the church comes into existence.

The images of the poor and needy, the resistant and dangerous, have forced ministry teams to look toward kingdom activities as a way of breaking through restrictions on mission activity. These causes have significant "market appeal" to the North American audience. But if we only engage in kingdom activities because of danger or poverty, what of those who are neither poor nor reactionary? More than half of the world's population is urban, without need of more hospitals or businesses, and who are not persecuting Christians. They still desperately need the kingdom. The sophisticated, the highly educated and the pampered are as needy as the poor and militant. What of the highly motivated businesspeople who know nothing of kingdom values by which to run their businesses? What about densely populated urban areas where community development is impossible, but crime is out of control?

If the slider switches are held in tension, whether we are working in a resistant area or not, the ministry team will seek to bring people into the church activities and help them to see that they are seated at the right hand of the King of kings, with the King's mandate to transform society and redeem culture.

EXAMPLES OF KEEPING THE END IN MIND

Following are some illustrations of what happens when disciples keep the end in mind, balancing the slider switches of church and kingdom.

Church as disciple-making school. Dallas Willard has said that the role of the church is to be a school of disciple making, so that disciples can live for the King in whatever domain of activity and influence they have.[15] The King rules through everyone who is serving him, regardless of the activity involved, a radical reversal of many default settings. Christ the King, seated on the throne, exercises his domain through all those who have acknowledged him as King and are serving him as King in *whatever circle of influence* he has given them.

Healing body and soul. Hospitals begun for the purpose of mission provide a wonderful example of maintaining the tension between word and works, church and kingdom. TEAM has had the privilege of partnering with an amazing hospital in the Middle East. When the hospital began over forty years ago, the rate of tuberculosis (TB) was high and getting higher. Drug-resistant strains of the disease were emerging. The nomadic and seminomadic population of the area had little access to medical care. TB silently killed many. Two amazing women, one a doctor and the other a nurse, decided that Jesus had called them to do something, so they moved to a small town at the edge of the desert and began to work. They were not satisfied, however, with curing TB. They were passionate about declaring the good news of the coming King, Jesus Christ. Every day they invited the patients to join them for healing for their souls through the Word of God.

To be sure, the hospital has been pulled and pushed over the years to do one or the other. At one point, local government police came to the hospital and told the director that they appreciated the medical work but the doctors had to stop telling people about Jesus. The director refused, declaring, "If I can't preach the gospel in this hospital, then I personally will blow it up." Apparently they had some construction going on at the time, and her statement was not just a threat. The official backed down.

A pediatrician who worked at this hospital put it this way, "We can send someone home from this hospital healed of drug-resistant tuberculosis, but if we have done nothing to heal the soul, they will still die one day, but without hope." One woman came to the clinic for a visit twenty years after being healed from TB. When she met the director she said, "Ever since I was here and the blood of Jesus took away my sin, I have been walking with him like this," holding up two intertwined fingers. Both her body and her soul had been healed.

They have kept the two slider switches in constant tension for over forty years. As a result, there are many disciples of Jesus scattered through this resistant region. The love of Christ has taken root. At the same time, the incidence of TB in the region has fallen dramatically. The impact of serving body and soul is being felt throughout the region.

Fighting for truth as well as justice. In the early '90s, South Africa was on the brink of civil war. The era of apartheid had officially ended in 1990 and, in the build-up to the elections of 1994, the ominous specter of civil war threatened. At that time a call to prayer went out to churches across the country. Church members may still have been meeting in denominations shaped by apartheid, but they were all bringing their prayers in unity before the King of the universe. He answered their prayers.

With the peaceful election of Nelson Mandela in 1994, many hoped that life would be different, but years of oppression do not easily lead toward peace. At a critical moment, Archbishop Desmond Tutu, at the request of President Mandela, organized the first truth and reconciliation commissions with a startling premise: any victims who would tell their story honestly and openly would receive recompense, and any perpetrators who would tell their story honestly and openly would receive amnesty.[16] Instead of taking revenge on perpetrators of injustice and violence, they invited them to confess publicly, and offered them freedom. The church, represented by Archbishop Desmond Tutu, brought kingdom values into society. Miraculously, not only did they avert a bloody and potentially devastating civil war, they effected a good beginning at overcoming the brutal results of decades of darkness.

Seeking the peace of the city together. Cathleen Lawler lives and works in Clovis, California, amid the great central valley that provides fruits and vegetables for the whole country. Clovis is changing rapidly, becoming increasingly plagued with the common problems of growing cities: unemployment, poverty, crime, drugs, violence and lack of good education. As part of a doctoral program, Cathleen interviewed ten ministry leaders from churches across the city as well as city leaders. She had a vision to find ways in which churches could work with each other and with the city leaders to "meet the needs of the community together."[17]

She discovered that the pastors were concerned about the city, and their respective churches were each trying to do something of benefit, but they had yet to collaborate with each other. Furthermore, she found that the projects the churches were doing separately did not align with the priorities of the city leaders themselves. Even though everyone was concerned about the same problems and wanted to collaborate, they were not working together toward a solution.

When she began to research the cause of the disparity between what leaders desired and actual practice, she discovered that most of the pastors simply ran into the problem of limited resources: time, budget and personnel. Although they wanted to collaborate, the demands of running the programs in each church made doing so very difficult.

Following the completion of her dissertation, Cathleen began networking with city and church leaders, trying to overcome the isolation. In response to prayer, God gave her an ally in the police force. Kelly, a police officer, had been given the responsibility of developing community relations, particularly in the most difficult areas of the city. She and Cathleen began working together. Normally, the only ones who see the police are the criminals, not the victims. Choosing an apartment complex with high crime rates, they decided to connect with the victims of crime, especially the 40 percent under the age of eight. They planned an *un-birthday* party for the community.

One Friday, a sunny, hot afternoon in Clovis, twenty police officers, including the chief of police, came out to flip burgers, play basketball with the children and show off the fire trucks. Kids could borrow books from a moving library, join a boys' club and eat cotton candy.

Kelly had contacted all of the churches on Cathleen's list to ask for their participation. Although none of the churches responded officially, a few of Cathleen's personal friends from those churches arrived to help. Several Hispanic churches also joined the party. The next time, Cathleen and Kelly want to ask pastors to give them names of specific individuals within their congregations who would have a heart to join them. They might even invite the pastors to spiritually commission those volunteers to help with the work begun by the police department.

Because of Cathleen's work, collaboration between multiple churches and city leaders has a more than better chance of making lasting changes to the problems that plague the city and the region. In the process, disciples of Jesus will have the opportunity to love their neighbors, to engage in real-life conversations and to point the way to the true author of peace.

Instead of letting the default settings stay in place, with each church group working independently, they are beginning to work together to bring the peace of the kingdom to the city. Instead of competition, they are engaging in collaboration, keeping the end in mind.

Disciples Keep the End in Mind

If someone joins a sports team, the end goal in mind is to win. For a business leader, the end is to make money and expand. For the church, the end is to exalt the King and to extend his kingdom to the uttermost parts of the earth by making disciples of all nations. That is the end against which church activities and life must be measured. That is the end disciples must keep in mind.

All of the previous principles combine toward this end. Letting God lead, learning to hear and obey, developing interdependent relationships, doing what love requires, making disciples, equipping disciples, living an undivided life and engaging in personal and cultural transformation—all are necessary to serve the King of kings and to seek his kingdom.

Disciples Organize Flexibly and Purposefully

Relationships and Organization

Being built together into a dwelling of God in the Spirit.

EPHESIANS 2:22

Early in my tenure as the international director of TEAM, I read the book *Orbiting the Giant Hairball: A Corporate Fool's Guide to Surviving with Grace*.[1] The author, Gordon MacKenzie, worked in the creative card division of the mega-company Hallmark Cards.

MacKenzie explores the paradox between creativity and organizational structure. Working alone, he could produce amazingly creative greeting cards, but without the organizational structure of Hallmark Cards to produce, market and sell them, very few people would ever buy one. On the other hand, the organizational structure itself had a tendency to suck out all creativity by standardizing processes. In his metaphor, the hairball is the sum of all the standardized policies and procedures necessary to run the company. The trick for a creative artist is to stay in orbit around it. If the hairball gets too large, its gravity draws all creativity into itself. If the hairball is not big enough, nothing is accomplished.

A similar paradox applies to the church. When two or three disciples gather in his name, Jesus is among them. This spiritual relational entity is, quite literally, the body of Christ, capable of discerning and carrying out the will of God in the world. In order to gather together, however, those disciples have to decide when, where and how to do so, requiring organization. As time goes on and the number of disciples who gather increases, necessary organization grows into organizational structure. The organizational structure exists to flexibly serve, nurture and enhance the spiritual relational entity—the body of Christ, collectively capable of carrying out God's will.

If the organizational structure becomes more important than the body of Christ within it, then the body may slowly die, even as the structure carries on. If the church becomes so highly organized that relationships become secondary and collective obedience is predetermined by the program, then it is in trouble. While the body cannot exist without organization, clearly the organization can exist without the body of Christ present. Some of the most ornate buildings in the world are church buildings in Europe, and many of them still have programs operating within, but the body of Christ is absent. Tourists who float in and out are the new "congregation."

Organizational structures must change and adjust whenever necessary to serve the body, not the other way around. Disciples organize flexibly and purposefully.

For the body of Christ to function, it must be built on relationships formed by deep bonds of friendship, time, trust, intimacy and love. In Spanish, this idea is captured in the word *confianza,* defined as trust that forms over long periods of time because of increasing intimacy. Relationships are tough, organic, emotional and lasting.

The defining value of relationships is belonging. The individual "belongs" in his or her family, neighborhood, community, team, workplace or church. He or she is accepted, loved, cared for and supported. This interconnected web of disciples who join one another on the same spiritual journey—following Jesus, learning of Jesus, loving each other and encouraging one another in the process—become the body of Christ, capable of carrying out the will of Christ in the world.

The question again is one of dynamic tension. Does necessary organization serve to make disciples, call them to be on mission together, nourish, and promote the growing maturity of the relational body of Christ within it? Or do the organizational structures smother, encrust or ignore the body? In the daily expectation of running a church and maintaining the programs, how healthy is the body of Christ?

When the organizational slider switch is set all the way to the top and the relational slider switch is all the way to the bottom, individual belonging is sacrificed for the good of the institution.

When the relational slider switch is set all the way to the top, however, and there is very little organizational structure, people may enjoy one another immensely, but little gets done—the purpose of accomplishing something together is lost.

MAINTAINING BIBLICAL TENSION: RELATIONSHIPS AND ORGANIZATION

All the metaphors that Paul uses in the book of Ephesians assume relationships between believers with Jesus in the center. Love is the operating principle. When love is present, God himself dwells in their midst. Love cannot operate outside relationships any more than yeast can work properly without dough.

Read the following passages; then read just the italicized words in sequence:

So then *you are* no longer strangers and aliens, but you are *fellow citizens* with the saints, and are *of God's household*, having been built on the foundation of the apostles and prophets, Christ Jesus Himself being the corner stone, in whom the whole building, being fitted together, is *growing into a holy temple in the Lord*, in whom you also are being built together into *a dwelling of God in the Spirit*. (Eph 2:19-22)

But speaking the truth in love, we are to grow up in all aspects into Him who is the head, even Christ, from whom *the whole body*, being fitted and held together by what every joint supplies, according to the proper working of each individual part, *causes the growth of the body* for the building up of itself in love. (Eph 4:15-16)

So that Christ may dwell in your hearts through faith; and that you, being rooted and grounded in love, may be able to comprehend with all the saints what is the breadth and length and height and depth, and to know the love of Christ which surpasses knowledge, *that you may be filled up to all the fullness of God*. (Eph 3:17-19)

These phrases have a relational essence, exquisitely organized under the headship of Christ, breathing in his presence and exhaling it in love to one another and to the world. Believers quiver with excitement at the notion of being a part of the body, eagerly anticipating being connected, so that the love of Christ can flow outward through them. The God of all creation wants to dwell in and among his people. How did this astonishing, world-transforming potential get reduced to the phrase, "go to church on Sunday"?

According to Paul, the body of Christ moves forward under the leadership of the apostles, prophets, evangelists, pastors and teachers (relational slider switch), and they manage the necessary organization through the offices of elders and deacons (organizational slider switch). A lot of ink has been spilled debating organizational structures—Presbyterian, Anglican, Lutheran, Baptist and so on. The key to this debate is to ask, What organizational structure is necessary for growing and maturing the body of Christ at this moment in time, in this culture, in this place in the world?

Each of these diverse church structures has been variously useful at different times and in different cultural contexts. Any organizational structure, however, has to be measured against the qualitative functions of the body of Christ—making disciples of Jesus, developing leaders who make disciples, following him on mission wherever he leads and deepening relationships.

Cultural Assumptions About Time and Organization

For a couple of years, Kris and I were part of a growing multiethnic congregation led by two pastors, one black, one white. In order to work through some of the inevitable issues that arose, I was invited to be part of a multiethnic strategic planning group. One night we evaluated the programs operating in the church, including the newly minted small group program launched by a white intern from a nearby seminary.

By this time, we had established enough confidence that all the participants were willing to share their thoughts honestly. The African American participants were puzzled at the small group program—they didn't understand the need at all. I remember asking, "Do you get together with one another regularly?" They responded, "Of course we do. We drop in on one another all the time!" "But do you talk about the Bible and pray?" "Sure. Don't you?" they asked.

The whites needed a schedule developed by the church to invest in relationships. The African Americans couldn't imagine the need for a program to do what they did naturally. The program would probably have inhibited the relational spiritual connections they already enjoyed. From their point of view, the program was a crutch—unnecessary for healthy relationships.

Programs and schedules are directly linked to another universal of worldview: time.

Every culture develops commonly agreed upon assumptions about time, including cyclical, pendular, episodic, linear and event time. These can be focused on the future, present or past. To understand the importance of these views in the life of the church, I'm going to highlight just two of these: future linear time and present event time.

Future linear time is broken uniformly into years, months, days, hours, minutes and seconds. Time is limited; each chunk of time is worth exactly as much as any equivalent chunk. For those with this worldview, time is money. One can save time, spend time, buy time, waste time, use time or invest time. An individual only spends time for something he or she values, spending greater amounts of time for something of greater value. Since time is money, punctuality is important. A person who doesn't arrive at an appointed time steals time from those who do.

Linear time moves forward into the future. Planning ahead has high value; spontaneity has low value. "Proper planning prevents poor performance." The further into the future something is planned, the more binding it is. Goals are set for future dates, and time is spent accordingly with the purpose of achieving something by that date.

In this worldview, time is like an expressway, and the exit is the future destination. No one is particularly interested in the scenery on the way—the important thing is to arrive at the exit. The intern in our multiethnic church was using linear time to organize a program with the future goal of producing healthy relationships.

Present event time occurs when people who know one another gather to do something together. Event time begins when people arrive and ends when everyone leaves. During the event the clock has no meaning or importance; linear time is suspended. A person who arrives when everyone else arrives is on time, regardless of the clock.

Event time operates in the present. Future appointments are backup plans in case something more interesting does not occur when the future date becomes the present. In contrast to the metaphor of an expressway, present event time is like a forest preserve trail that begins and ends at the same place. The point of walking along the trail is to be with others, enjoying their company. The African Americans in our strategic planning group (note the irony) operated with one another using present event time, dropping in on one another spontaneously.

In Afghanistan, disciples cannot gather in public places for large gatherings because of the risk to their lives. They gather in small cells of two or three people, meeting in teashops or on the street. They also meet in households. These gatherings are not structured around the clock; no program requires them to meet—they happen spontaneously and organically. In this sense the church is similar to the African Americans who dropped in on one another. The church in Afghanistan is growing and it is healthy. These groups are operating on event time.

Discussing this one day with others on this disciple-making journey, one said, "It seems as if these cells and households are the essentials. If you can gather in larger groups, such as missional communities and crowd gatherings, it's a bonus. But if all you have are the latter, you're probably in trouble."

Movements versus institutions. Hirsch makes the comment, "We must find a new way to experience ourselves, beyond the static, mechanistic, and institutional paradigm that predominates in our ecclesial life."[2] In order to find a way beyond the "progressively more machinelike apparatus required to 'run a church,'" Hirsch turned to something called a *living systems approach*,[3] or what many are calling *movements*.

In a movement, leaders organize life as it arises, letting God lead, hearing and obeying what he says (two principles of disciple making). Consistent development of principles of discipleship is necessary in order for the body of Christ to grow and develop as an organic movement. As it grows and develops, different programs and organization will be necessary and appropriate. In an institution, leaders may try to create growth by planning and organizing toward that end, rather than responding to life that grows organically.

Simplifying dramatically, as a child grows his or her clothes change accordingly. As the child becomes an adult, the clothes are reflective of the maturity of the individual and the activity in which he or she is engaged. A football player, for instance, becomes a football player through rigorous exercise and practice; the uniform is appropriate and necessary to play the game. But putting a uniform on someone does not make him a football player, just as putting adult pants on a child does not make the child an adult. Programs, like clothes, are necessary, but they have to change and adjust according to the needs of the living entity, the body of Christ.

Movements apparently are more likely to thrive in collective cultures that function on event time. Very few, if any, of the flourishing disciple-making movements in the world today are in individualist cultures that utilize linear time.[4] In these cultures, institutions function as convenient places for individuals to gather whether they know one another or not.

Institutions do a tremendous amount of good in the world. No country can flourish without solid institutions providing government, education, transportation, health care and so forth. Many Christian institutions have contributed an enormous amount of good for the kingdom. Publishing houses, hospitals and schools are among countless institutions that do good, and without them the world would be a very sad place.

The body of Christ, however, is not an institution. It might be carried and nurtured within an institution, but the two are different. When the church functions exclusively like an institution, the body suffers.

The expression "go to church" embodies institutional assumptions. Church is a *property* where we go to attend a *program*, led by those who have vested *power*. The property, programs and power structures may be large and complex, or small and simple, but they are the defining features of an institution. The individuals who "go to church" are the congregation. They will continue to go as long as the institution meets their individual needs, and they may even mix and match: preaching from one church, fellowship from another, youth program from a third (consumerism).

As an institution, a church can develop a life of its own, regardless of the needs of the body within it. Once a given church develops a particular set of programs, then the congregation learns that to be faithful to the Lord, the programs must continue to run. If someone proposes a change in program, the change not only influences individual decisions about whether to stay or not, it actually threatens their very notion of what the church is about and what it means to be faithful to Christ.

In the mid-'90s, I consulted with a church that was undergoing a change in pastoral leadership. They created a strategic planning committee and asked me to lead. During our work, we created a list of all the programs that were running in the church. We listed 125 different programs, including twenty-five committees that were necessary to keep the rest of the programs running. This particular church is in an area where people travel during the summer or take long weekends at various vacation cottages. Due to the lack of volunteers, running all the programs during the summer was increasingly difficult. Those who did volunteer ended up carrying an inordinate amount of the load, wearing out in the process, often becoming disillusioned.

We recommended that the leadership clarify their vision for the body, keep the programs that were helping them accomplish their vision, drop the ones that were no longer necessary, and add new programs if needed. We also recommended that they dramatically diminish the number of programs they were running during the summer. They tabled the findings of the committee when they hired a new pastor.

About fifteen years later I met with the pastor for coffee. He said, "I've been able to add some things that the church needed, but I have not been able to stop anything." The long list of 125 programs had actually increased. For many people, the programs *were* the church.

I have no idea how many programs the average church runs. Hopefully the case mentioned is an extreme. But I have come to believe that unless programs have a built-in sunset provision and are evaluated each year against the core functions of the body of Christ, they will become impossible to change. When people associate their faithfulness to God and the body of Christ with a given program, change becomes extremely difficult, if not impossible. The means become the end. Changing the programs is tantamount to changing their relationship with God, even if those programs may not be helping achieve the original vision for which they were started.

As international director of TEAM, I would often lead prayer and vision retreats with our missionaries in different countries. In one such retreat, after we had clarified the vision to which the Lord was leading us, I asked the fourteen people assembled for a list of activities or programs in which they were involved. We listed thirty-five different activities (programs). Then I asked them to add to the list any activities they had not yet tried but which would help them achieve their vision. They added fifteen more. Now we had a list of fifty activities among fourteen people. Finally, I asked each one to pray through the list and to choose fourteen activities that would be most helpful to achieve what they believed God wanted them to do—each had fourteen votes, so to speak.

After prayerful, thoughtful evaluation, we tallied the list. It was immediately obvious which activities would help them accomplish their vision. Most of them had chosen many of the same items out of fifty possible activities—some items actually had fourteen votes, while many had none. I thought it would be simple to discontinue the ones that had few or no votes, but one participant remarked, "I didn't choose those because I thought they were given." Nothing changed immediately. Years later, however, through hard work by some of the leaders, the activities were readjusted toward the vision.

Perhaps even more deceptive than programs is the lure of buildings and property. During 120 years of its existence, TEAM acquired property throughout the world. We did it honestly and with the best intentions. But sooner or later, the property that we acquired almost inevitably became a handicap.

We should remember that the Sermon on the Mount (or collection of sermons) actually took place outside of a building, and when Jesus preached the parables of the kingdom, he did it from a boat. When organizational structures grow, they subtly but easily begin to create competition with the kingdom.

The needs of the institution can all too easily outweigh the purpose for which the believers have organized in the first place—to be the body of Christ and to carry out his will. Instead of bending all our efforts toward the kingdom, we begin to waste our energies preserving our kingdoms.

EXAMPLES OF ORGANIZING LIFE TOGETHER

Adjusting activities with the purpose in mind. In Venezuela, TEAM worked with two associations of churches, one on the eastern side of the country (inherited from a merger with Orinoco River Mission) and one on the western. Both associations were birthed through missionary efforts. Toward the end of the twentieth century, each association numbered over three hundred churches, Venezuelans were leading the churches and each association had a Bible institute for training its own leadership.

During the decade of the '80s, TEAM handed over the ownership and responsibility for several institutions we had created to the corresponding church associations. These institutions included three bookstores, a publishing house, two Bible institutes, correspondence schools and a three-story office and apartment complex. We turned over a seminary to our partners, the Evangelical Free Church Mission and their Venezuelan church association. Without demanding any remuneration, we handed over properties, buildings, material and mailing lists. We sold the three-story office and apartment complex for one dollar to serve as the headquarters of the western church association. All in all, we thought we had done a fine thing. We had certainly avoided possibly acrimonious debates about power and control. We congratulated ourselves that we had worked ourselves out of a job, trusting the Venezuelan church leaders.

Then during the '90s, slowly but surely the institutions we turned over began to falter. I clearly remember one discussion about the Bible institute in the east. The mission was no longer in control, but the school was still dependent on funds that came through TEAM. Unfortunately, TEAM no longer had enough funds to cover the increasing deficit. Missionaries who had given blood, sweat and tears for that institution were devastated. After a further year of struggle, the Bible institute closed.

Then an amazing thing happened. Several of the eastern church leaders said, "We can't stop training leaders just because the Bible institute is no longer able to function—let's figure out another way." They met with a couple of TEAM missionaries and began to rethink the entire method of training leaders. Eventually they designed a strategy in which they would gather church leaders for one Saturday a month in different locations, using various buildings available to the churches. Each month they would focus on one of seven key areas of growth. Pastors and church leaders could immediately put into practice what they learned during the Saturday sessions.

The leaders created a well-designed program to accomplish leadership training. Churches began to thrive and multiply because the new method could supply pastors as fast as they were needed for new congregations. The church leaders flexibly and purposefully reorganized themselves to continue to develop leaders.

Organizing just enough. As this method of leadership training began to develop momentum, one of the pastors created a "work plan" for his church. According to his work plan, everyone in the church needed to know how to evangelize and how to make disciples. Assuming they learned these two things, they would then need to learn how to carry out other responsibilities in the church, such as teaching, leading or managing. Finally, those who rose through these levels of training would be invited to the monthly pastoral training sessions.

To launch this multilevel work plan, he announced to his church that they were going to take an evangelism vacation together (*vacaciónes evangelísticas*) in a designated town where there was one small church. He invited everyone who wanted to participate to take their vacation during the same week in that town, stay for the week and visit people in the community. Beyond that announcement, no further planning took place.

On the appointed week, a few dozen people from his church rolled up their hammocks and traveled to the town indicated. When they got there, everyone worked together to find a place to hang their hammocks. Spontaneously they decided what and when to eat. Then they began visiting the people in the community, sharing their stories, talking about Jesus and inviting people to join the small church that already existed. Lives changed, others began following Jesus and by the end of the week, dozens of new people began attending the church. With the thrill of seeing people come to Christ, they experienced the best vacation ever.

They raised no funds, had no budget, built no buildings. They did not create an institution for evangelism. By knowing when and where to arrive, they had organized their activities just enough to carry out the task at hand. With this simple act of obedience, the pastor launched his multilevel work plan. Now he knew which people to train in disciple making, which to invite into leadership and whom to bring to the monthly pastors' training event.

Other churches in the vicinity of his church began to hear of his work plan, and they wanted to try it. The idea began to jump across denominational boundaries, and churches from other backgrounds began using the same work plan. They began identifying with one another, demonstrating even in church names that all the different denominations were part of the same body of Christ in the city or town in which they were located. The churches in eastern Venezuela began to expand spontaneously. As new churches were born, leadership was ready to take their place within them because they had been brought up through the various levels of the work plan.

Staying flexible. When the Berlin Wall came down, TEAM joined other agencies to train Russians to start churches throughout their own country. TEAM recruited seasoned workers, all of whom had a good track record in making disciples, to move to Moscow and participate. Together with our partners, the workers organized week-long seminars in Moscow where leaders gathered to receive training in starting and growing churches. The TEAM workers, however, decided that they were not going to invest in any property in Moscow. They would rent apartments and use public transportation.

The training seminars made use of rented facilities and the program remained flexible. After some experimentation, they changed their method of training to include more imitation through mentoring. The team decided to start a church themselves, working with students, learning together. Because the organizational structures with which they were working were still fluid and flexible, the team dropped their rentals, moved to an unreached area of Russia and began working there. The workers made a covenant with each other to pray together every day at noon for a half hour, and to seek to share Jesus with someone daily. This simple level of organization had a powerful effect. Without buying any property, a group of disciples formed within less than a year. Even when one member of the team was taken hostage and the team disbanded, the body of Christ carried on making disciples and producing leaders. Over half of the members of that small church went on to become leaders in other parts of the country.

They never allowed the organizational structures to supersede the purpose for which they were called. They continued to organize flexibly and purposefully.

Emphasizing the essentials. I was five years old when the knock came on the courtyard gate. Our small whitewashed house had four rooms all in a row, with doors between and a porch along the front. A stone wall enclosed a small courtyard in front of the porch. The Himalayan Mountains soared into the blue hazy distance behind our house. On a clear day we could see the snow-drenched, ice-carved peaks.

That night, Dad got up and went to the gate where he stayed for a long time. When he came back, he gathered the family together and told us that Ahmet had just come by. Ahmet's father found out that he was studying the Bible and was trying to find him to shoot him with his rifle. Ahmet had decided to run away to one of the big cities where his father would not be able to find him. We prayed for Ahmet but we never heard from him again. I came face-to-face with the cost of committing one's life to Christ, and never forgot it.

Often we commiserate with those who work in Muslim countries because the work is so hard and the results seem so meager. Only recently have I realized that the Muslim world creates a context where, specifically because we are without the benefit of large organizational programs, buildings or institutions, we are forced to make disciples in some of the best and most powerful ways possible. Research carried out by Fuller Seminary has been tracking the amazing growth of the body of Christ in the Muslim world.[5] Stories continue to emerge of thousands of believers in Afghanistan, Bangladesh and Iran, some of the most difficult places in the world.

The Muslim context forces us to recognize the potential of training others and developing leaders who in turn develop other leaders, rather than the missionary retaining control or power. When the missionary equips disciples to minister with their spiritual gifts for the benefit and spiritual growth of still others, then the group does not become dependent on the outsider. The parable of the leaven and the parable of the mustard seed both make the same point. The dough becomes leavened not by some mastermind chemist who needs equipment and training, but because the leaven quietly and simply multiplies, over and over again. The mustard seed becomes a large tree in the same way.

Three TEAM colleagues visited a household church in a Muslim country torn apart by more than thirty years of war. After a delicious meal of curry and rice, the young father hosting the meal was asked to lead the group in sharing the Lord's Supper together. As he ripped the bread in two, reciting the well-known passage from 1 Corinthians 11, no one had any doubt what it meant to put their lives on the line to follow Jesus. Nor did anyone doubt that the meaning of the event was even greater because he had led the sacred meal rather than the missionary.

If new believers think that they must have a building in order to have a church, then the church can only grow as fast as they can buy or build new buildings. Inevitably, the walls of the new building become the limit for how far or fast the church can grow. If the church must have a seminary-trained pastor, then the church can only grow as fast as seminary-trained pastors become available. If the church must have an elaborate sound system in order to worship, then the church can only grow as fast as they are able to purchase sound systems. But when the church understands, as they do in the Muslim context, that it is composed of believers committed to learning of and obeying the Lord together, then it has the potential for shaking off obstacles and growing far beyond our imagination.

DISCIPLES ORGANIZE FLEXIBLY AND PURPOSEFULLY

The body of Christ is a beautiful, powerful creation of God. Institutions and organizations can serve it, but no institution can contain it. The measure of its health is found in these disciple-making principles. Does the body know how to let God lead? Do the disciples, individually and collectively, listen, discern his will and obey? Do they develop relational interdependence? Do they do what love requires? Do they know how to make disciples and equip them for ministry?

Changes in activities, programs and organizational structures should serve these ends. When they do, we begin to catch glimpses of the body of Christ at work.

12

Glimpses of a Disciple-Making Community

So that the manifold wisdom of God might now be
made known through the church to the rulers
and the authorities in the heavenly places.

EPHESIANS 3:10

When it functions the way God intended, with Jesus as Lord, the body of Christ dazzles our minds and hearts. Whether a fleeting glimpse into the throne room itself, a moment of shared intimacy with a person radically different, a simple prayer for safety—the body, functioning under the headship of Christ, changes lives irrevocably.

THE VIEW FROM THE THRONE ROOM

In the letter to the Ephesians, Paul traces an astonishing rescue taking place as Jesus redeems individuals, builds his disciples into one body and raises that body to his side in the heavenly places where he is seated beside the Father, with every power in heaven and on earth beneath his feet.

In the late '90s one of our workers was taken hostage by a terrorist organization in southern Russia. Walking home one evening after playing basketball with some orphan kids, he was suddenly surrounded by two thugs and bundled into a large white car. TEAM's crisis management policy immediately kicked in, requiring that any family members be evacuated, so as not to give the hostage takers an emotional advantage in the ensuing negotiations. Within two days, his wife was seated in an airplane, cruising at 36,000 feet above the Atlantic, moving farther and farther away from her husband, wherever he was.

In that moment of excruciating personal crisis, she decided to close her eyes and listen to some worship music, putting a cassette tape into her tape player. She had heard the music dozens of times before, but this time was different. As she began to worship, to her wonder the door of heaven opened and she was invited into the throne room. The light, joy, music, color and glory were overwhelming. Tears began streaming down her face. It was like the best party ever! Physically, she was sitting in the economy seat of an airplane. Spiritually, she was seeing what Paul,[1] Ezekiel,[2] Isaiah[3] and John[4] had seen.

She was not alone. She had joined the body of Christ around the throne of God. Thousands of believers around the world were also present in that throne room through their prayers, seeking the power of almighty God on their behalf.

She had a glimpse of the eternal, invisible God. Later, she said that if heaven was that glorious, she wondered why we grieved when our saved loved ones died. Rather, we should be dancing with joy that another one has been given the privilege of joining the party. When the tape reached the end and snapped off, the door to heaven closed, but not before she knew, "It's going to be okay."

In the ensuing months, to those working for his release, the dark, drawn-out process of negotiations with the hostage takers seemed endless, potentially devastating emotionally. The view from the throne room was altogether different. He was in control. All things would work out for the good he proposed to accomplish, redeeming the evil. No one was beyond his reach. His very presence reached into the small room in which her husband was kept.

Seven and a half months later her husband was released. He had lost a finger but was virtually unharmed emotionally and spiritually, without paying a ransom—a modern-day miracle.

Obviously, this kind of event is exceedingly rare. But what is not rare is the power that flows from the throne room at the request of the body of Christ.

Multicultural, Multiethnic by Design

The great reunion around the throne of God at the end of time will not be divided into race, language, class or ethnicity.

The unthinkable had happened. Those who hated each other for centuries, who had been taught not to touch each other, who could not enter one another's homes, whose foods were forbidden to each other, could be completely united in Christ as one body. That bond superseded every other source of identity. A Jew and a Gentile could embrace, pray together, worship together, drink from the same cup, work together, go on mission together, serve God together. In every way that mattered, they were one and at peace with each other. This incredible truth—the "manifold wisdom of God"—overturned centuries of animosity and law.

If Jew and Gentile could live and work in peace with each other, then any animosity that exists in the world can be overcome by the love of Christ at work in his body. While director of TEAM, I had the opportunity to travel to more than thirty-five countries of the world. I quickly discovered that no matter where one travels on the planet, people have learned to hate those next door: Pakistanis and Indians; Uzbeks and Tajiks; northern Italians and southern Italians; Colombians and Venezuelans; migrant Javanese and native Papuans;

Hutus and Tutsies; Sunni and Shia—just to name a few. All have learned to fear and hate each other, tearing the world apart with anger, war, racism, cruelty and genocide.

If the manifold wisdom of God could bring Jews and Gentiles together into one body, then any warring groups can be transformed by being drawn into the body of Christ, becoming one. Class and gender distinctions also disappear: upper caste and lower caste, rich and poor, male and female, free and slave. All can be transformed into one body by the blood of Jesus Christ who makes "both groups into one . . . thus establishing peace" (Eph 2:14-16).

While working in Caracas, we developed a vision to reach middle-class Venezuelans, one of the least reached groups in Venezuela. Our team began to make contacts, start small groups and invite people to study the Bible with us. Eventually we saw some people commit their lives to following Jesus, but they were not just middle-class Venezuelans. Colombians, Peruvians and Haitians also joined us, as well as some whose income was much less than middle-class professionals. In some ways we almost felt abashed that our goal of reaching middle-class Venezuelans was being diluted, when in reality a miracle was actually taking place before our eyes. The manifold wisdom of God was playing out in front of us. Colombians and Venezuelans, rich and poor were learning to love each other. God was doing more than we could imagine.

The manifold wisdom of God overturns the one thing that no power on earth is capable of overturning: pride and hatred of one group toward another. No peace plan between the Palestinians and Israelis will work until the body of Christ grows among them. No plan for reconciliation between Japanese and Chinese will work until they turn to the one who can make peace through his blood.

But manifold wisdom is not just about reconciliation or the absence of animosity. Being one means that we will finally become complete once more.

Take language as an example: When the people of the world were cursed at the Tower of Babel and divided, each family or race that had been a part of the whole would now labor to develop language and culture without the richness and fullness of all the different parts. One world language was broken up like so many slices of pie. The Germans received the guttural sounds, the South Africans the clicks, the Spanish the softness of the tip of the tongue and lips, the Chinese the musical tones. Each race or family had to make do with just what it had. But imagine putting it all back together again, when all will be able to use the best expression from any language. Imagine completely effective communication.

During the twentieth century missionaries came to believe that if we gathered homogenous people together, the church would grow faster. Surely bigger churches were better than smaller ones. They reasoned pragmatically that people from one class or caste or ethnicity would not want to become Christians if doing so meant they had to join a church that consisted primarily of the other class, caste or ethnicity. Church growth became an end in itself, and the manifold wisdom of God took a back seat.

The homogenous unit principle made some sense as a strategic entry point for evangelism, and in some places in the world, simple isolation or language differences might force one group to be homogenous. But when it becomes characteristic of the global body of Christ, the homogenous unit principle categorically contradicts Scripture. If Paul had believed in this principle, he would have had Jewish congregations and Gentile congregations, and the good news of the manifold wisdom of God would never have become apparent. John's vision—of men and women from every tribe, language, people and nation gathered together as one kingdom and priests to serve our God—would be false (Rev 5:9-10).

God never said that the bigger the church the better. If that were the case, then Jesus went sadly wrong when he offended the crowds and they ceased to follow him. When it comes to the body of Christ, *better* is defined as love and unity between vastly different human beings, male and female, rich and poor, Jew and Gentile, together as one body—truly the only solution for a broken planet.

During our second assignment in Venezuela, we lived in a government-subsidized housing development, occupying one half of a duplex. On the other side of the duplex lived a family that seemed to be shouting at one another constantly. The two young boys were wild. The father was a tall, black, muscular man who drove a truck for a living. Eventually his two sons participated in functions we had for children. One day he told us that he had had a meaningful spiritual experience at a different church and that he wanted to join us on a Sunday.

After a few years of work, the body of Christ was beginning to grow and thrive in our neighborhood, meeting on Sundays in our open garage area. We wanted the celebration of communion to be culturally appropriate, so we discussed the meaning with the first believers, asking their opinions on how to carry it out. Eventually we decided that we would use a common cup, filled with wine, with the option of individual communion cups for anyone who was sick or felt inhibited from taking a common cup. Small groups spontaneously gathered around the communion table, passing the cup from one to the other, saying, "This is the blood of Christ, shed for you."

One Sunday, as I moved to the front to form a small group for communion, I realized that my neighbor was standing right next to me. He received the cup from the person to his left, drank and then handed me the cup, saying the words, "This is the blood of Christ, shed for you." I took the cup from him and drank. Immediately, I was overwhelmed with a sense of profound oneness. We drank from the same cup. All the differences of race, culture, education, class, upbringing and occupation faded away as we shared the wine, as members of one body. I have celebrated communion many times in my life, but rarely as meaningfully as that Sunday.

Working through the principles contained in this book with people from different backgrounds can provide a path to that kind of unity. Few will disagree with the principles; the difficulty is in knowing how to turn them into action. To do that, we have to learn from one another with humility.

A DWELLING PLACE OF GOD

Salvation through Christ is our entrance ticket into the body where we are seated beside Christ,[5] at the right hand of God, the greatest force in the universe. Becoming part of the body of Christ is so much more than praying a prayer, becoming a Christian and playing church well. God actually carries out his will through his body.

The body of Christ has the power to provide a new culture and set of patterns that reflect the fruit of the Spirit. Hence, kindness can now become embedded in relationships as people meet for prayer and fellowship. Love becomes the operating system of the body, thinking of others first, seeking to meet their needs. Joy bubbles up when several members of the body get together. The body has the power to replace fear and worry with peace, where others are patient with weaknesses, while still being faithful to tell the truth.

These new patterns are the way in which the body of Christ is meant to function, leading Paul to grope for metaphors that stun us and fill us with hope: "fellow citizens with the saints . . . of God's household . . . a holy temple in the Lord . . . a dwelling of God in the Spirit" (Eph 2:19-22). Truly a solution for a broken world.

During Holy Week, many people participate in daily processions sponsored by local Catholic churches, beginning with Palm Sunday. Each day of the week a select group carries a large statue of Jesus through the streets depicting the scenes from Passion Week: Jesus before Pilate. Jesus being beaten. Jesus carrying the cross. Jesus on a cross. Friday marks the high point of the week as they carry a statue of Jesus dead in a glass enclosed coffin—the longest most solemn procession of the week. Then everyone goes home, or joins the rest of their friends on the beach. On Sunday everything is quiet: no public celebrations, no processions.

One year in Caracas as Easter approached, we decided to invite other churches with whom we had a relationship to join us in a march on Easter Sunday. We wanted everyone to know that Jesus had also risen from the dead and decided to have our own procession to celebrate. We created a huge banner, got permission from the local authorities for a particular area of the city, and prayed that it would not rain. About one hundred of us from several different churches gathered on Sunday afternoon in the parking lot of a local shopping mall. Then we marched to our predetermined destination, singing and waving.

Afterward about thirty of us from our congregation decided to meet at one of our homes for some refreshments and to have communion. As we passed around the bread and the wine, someone started singing the Lord's Prayer to a well-known tune. Somehow, without any previous decision, we found ourselves on our knees, singing our hearts out, hands lifted high, tears streaming down our faces. We felt that we were, at that moment in time, truly a "dwelling of God in the Spirit," we were "a holy temple in the Lord," proclaiming to anyone that would listen that Jesus was Lord, that he had been raised from the dead, that we were his followers. His manifold wisdom was being made known through the church.

Connected Through Prayer to the Power Center of the Universe

From the beginning, God set out to accomplish his eternal purpose of demonstrating to the universe, and to the spiritual powers that opposed his work, that with Jesus at the center, he could create a body that would be infinitely diverse, and yet be completely one in his presence.

We have been invited to enter the power center of the universe with boldness and confidence, because we have been united to Christ who has delivered us personally, called and gifted each of us and joined us to his body. All power flows from the almighty God: Father, Son and Spirit.

Together, led by the head of the body, his power flows through us as we go on mission to make disciples of the nations, calling on him to open up the way, defeating the forces arrayed against us, making us fruitful for the kingdom.

As we made disciples in our work in Caracas, we wanted to teach them how to listen to God and let him lead their prayers. We invited people to be silent, to listen to the Holy Spirit and to pray for whatever the Holy Spirit put in their hearts. One night, fifteen or twenty of us gathered in a small conference room designed for about twelve. The meeting started with multiple conversations as people caught up with one another, sharing their experiences of the week. After about twenty minutes, someone called out, "Time to pray." An expectant silence descended. Soon someone started praying, and another followed the conversation, and another and another. Then someone started singing one of the choruses or songs we knew as a body. Without any accompaniment, everyone joined in, and the prayer and singing continued until someone realized that we had to quit for the night. One woman sang in a monotone, clearly audible, her heart rejoicing and full of love for the Lord and those around her. In that small room with no electric guitars or drums, I have never known more moving worship, nothing more beautiful than those songs of worship from the heart, led by the unseen impulses of the Holy Spirit.

Throughout the centuries, the body of Christ has developed many different forms and practices of speaking with God. Prayer, in whatever form it takes, can move us together into the throne room. Our perspective changes. His authority begins to flow through us. The enemy trembles.

One evening in our home, we closed the discussion time and invited everyone to pray. Having new believers in the group, we again told people to listen to the Holy Spirit and to say whatever the Holy Spirit put into their hearts to pray. Then we waited. Several people prayed, including my wife, Kris. She prayed a simple prayer for Ivan, one of the new believers, asking the Lord to grant him safety in his weekly commute to the city of Valencia over a difficult, high-speed expressway. After several had prayed, we closed the time of prayer and invited people to share refreshments together.

Before we stood up, however, Ivan asked if he could say something. In a halting voice, he said that he had been trying to pray for safety on his weekly commute to Valencia, but each time he tried to say something, a lump came into his throat and he couldn't say the words. He said that just as he was giving up hope to be able to pray at all, he suddenly heard Kris praying for him, expressing exactly what was in his thoughts and mind. When he told us, we all stared in wonder. None of us doubted that the Holy Spirit had spoken through Kris. Many years later, I asked Ivan when he really knew that everything we believed was real. He related that incident.

That night in our living room, in a simple time of prayer, he came face-to-face with God's presence in his life, taking an unforgettable step forward in his journey of faith.

This throne room to which the body of Christ has "boldness and confident access, through faith in Him" is our birthright as children of God. From that position, seated with Christ at the right hand of the Father, the body of Christ takes on the broken world, incarnating the good news of the kingdom and breaking through the barriers set up by individual sin, cultural patterns and dark spiritual forces.

The body of Christ with Jesus as Lord—not playing church—is indeed, the best hope for the world.

Study Questions

by Dietrich Gruen

INTRODUCTION: MY JOURNEY AS DISCIPLE AND DISCIPLE MAKER

1. The author opens with a curious and courageous statement: "I am passionately in love with the body of Christ. That has not always been true." Does your journey reflect his in any significant ways?

2. What are the significant spiritual turning points in your journey as a disciple?

3. What does the author mean by universal disciple-making principles?

1 WHAT IS A DISCIPLE ANYWAY?

1. Define the word *disciple* the way you have understood it previously.

2. Which of the following descriptions resonate with you the most? The least?

   - Learners
   - Followers
   - Lovers
   - Of Jesus
   - Together

3. After listening carefully to the Spirit, what changes do you think Jesus wants you to make in your own life?

2 Disciples Let God Lead from the Invisible World

1. Assess where the slider switches for visible and invisible are currently set in your life, your church or ministry assignment. How sensitive or discerning are you to the presence of invisible good and the power of the Holy Spirit, or conversely, the presence of evil?

2. Think of some area of concern you have. What would need to take place in the "heavenly places" for your request to be granted?

Further reading:

Ruth Haley Barton, *Pursuing God's Will Together* (Downers Grove, IL: InterVarsity Press, 2012).

Reema Goode, *Which None Can Shut* (Carol Stream, IL: Tyndale House Publishers, 2010).

3 Disciples Hear and Obey

1. Assess where the two slider switches—knowledge and behavior—are currently set in your church or your ministry assignment.

2. In the spiritual turning points of your life as a disciple, what was the relationship between knowledge and behavior, respectively?

3. If you were to commit to doing whatever you are reasonably sure Jesus is saying, or the Holy Spirit is asking you to do, does that excite you? Scare you? Why?

Further reading:

Henri J. M. Nouwen, *The Return of the Prodigal Son* (New York: Doubleday, 1994).

Clare de Graaf, *The 10-Second Rule: Following Jesus Made Simple* (New York: Howard Books, 2010).

4 Disciples Develop Relational Interdependence

1. How would reintroducing healthy tension into this set of slider switches help you and your ministry?

2. Reorienting our perspective to allow for the plural in worship as we do in our prayers, what do we learn about our identity in Christ?

3. Think of three or four major decisions you have made in your life. How many were made based on the opinion of the group to which you belonged?

4. Consider how you might balance the slider switches to create interdependence:

   - Islands of timelessness

   - An open heart and door

   - Experiments in interdependency—borrowing, seeking advice in decision making

Further reading:

Robert N. Bellah et al., *Habits of the Heart: Individualism and Commitment in American Life* (New York: Harper & Row, 1985).

5 DISCIPLES DO WHAT LOVE REQUIRES

1. Assess your own default slider switch settings relative to word/ truth vs. works/justice. After listening carefully to the Spirit, what changes do you think Jesus wants you to make in your own life?

2. Imagine yourself among those who successfully befriend someone like Lisbeth for Christ to redeem the situation in which she is caught up. What would love require?

3. Reexamine the biblical examples of this gospel tension, cited by the author and relisted below, and ask yourself: Where on the slider switches of word and truth vs. works and justice would you rate each case?

   - The Samaritan woman (Jn 4:1-26)

   - The Jews at Pentecost (Acts 2:14-41)

- The Philippian jailer (Acts 16:16-34)
- The rich young ruler (Mt 19:16-29)
- The centurion under authority (Mt 8:5-13)
- The Ethiopian official (Acts 8:26-40)
- The two disciples on the road to Emmaus (Lk 24:13-35)

Further reading:
Brent Curtis and John Eldredge, *The Sacred Romance: Drawing Closer to the Heart of God* (Nashville, TN: Thomas Nelson, 1997).
Scot McKnight, *The Jesus Creed: Loving God, Loving Others* (Brewster, MA: Paraclete Press, 2004).

6 Disciples Make Disciples

1. In the spiritual turning points of your life, what was the role of preaching or lecturing in bringing about the change versus the role of mentoring or interaction with others?

2. Think of the people who have had a life-changing impact on you. What made that relationship meaningful and/or memorable?

3. How can you build such relationships into the fabric of your current ministry?

Further reading:
Dallas Willard, *The Spirit of the Disciplines: Understanding How God Changes Lives* (New York: HarperCollins, 1988).

7 Leaders Equip Disciples for Ministry

1. In his ministry in Maracay, Venezuela, the author formed a leadership team of four. Evaluating that team later, what was positive and what was negative?

2. What percent of members of your church or ministry are actively using their gifts? What would it take to increase the percentage?

3. The author compares the fivefold gifting (apostle, prophet, evangelist, pastor, teacher) to systems of the human body. By this five-system analogy, how would you assess the health of your congregation? What would it take to increase its health, making all five systems operational?

4. What lines are drawn between leaders and disciples where you belong and worship?

Further reading:
Roland Allen, *Missionary Methods: St. Paul's or Ours?* (Grand Rapids: Eerdmans, 1983).

8 DISCIPLES LIVE AN UNDIVIDED LIFE

1. How does your current church or ministry assignment compare to the statement, "The secular is the public space where government, education, business, law and communication exist and where spirituality and morality have no place. The sacred is the private, individual space where morality is determined and where individuals make personal faith decisions"?

2. The secular and sacred slider switches can be held in tension by asking the question, "What is my obedience to Christ in a particular situation?" Share with other believers any decisions you are facing and what you think Jesus wants you to do. Do other believers affirm what you think you have heard?

3. How would you answer the author's rhetorical question, *Where are the Sayerses, Dumases, Tolstoys, Bachs and Hugos today?*

4. How does this dichotomy play out in your intercultural experience?

   - Choice of schools (public vs. parochial)
   - Discretionary use of free time (dinner with non-Christian friends vs. a church-based Bible study)

- Church planting or outreach efforts (business as mission model vs. religious-use-only building vs. shared community space)

Further reading:

Dale Losch, *A Better Way: Make Disciples Wherever Life Happens* (Kansas City, MO: Crossworld, 2012).

9 DISCIPLES ENGAGE IN PERSONAL AND CULTURAL TRANSFORMATION

1. What do you find most radical or countercultural about the Sermon on the Mount (Lk 6:20-38)?

2. What cultural patterns around you most reflect the image of God?

3. What cultural patterns around you reflect the fallen nature of the human race?

4. What process do you find most useful for engaging in personal transformation?

Further reading:

Jerry Bridges, *Respectable Sins* (Colorado Springs, CO: NavPress, 2007).

10 DISCIPLES KEEP THE END IN MIND

1. How does your current church or ministry assignment compare to the slider switch settings of kingdom and church?

2. If you were the author, how would you answer the question posed to him: "Why do evangelicals do so little for the community? The Catholic church has all kinds of programs, but the evangelicals seem content with just going to church."

3. Where you live and work, what are some of the ways in which various evangelical groups or churches are working together for the good of the community or city?

Further reading:

E. Stanley Jones, *The Unshakable Kingdom and the Unchanging Person* (Nashville: Abingdon Press, 1972).

Hugh Halter and Matt Smay, *The Tangible Kingdom* (San Francisco: Jossey-Bass, 2008).

11 Disciples Organize Flexibly and Purposefully

1. Considering your experience in the church or ministry team, how do you know that the body of Christ is present?

2. What do you see in Paul's metaphors in Ephesians that reveals a high organizational setting? A high relational setting? Which metaphor engages your imagination?

3. Does your church or ministry team flexibly and purposefully manage programs? If so, how?

4. Considering the difference between an institution and a movement, what would it take for you to become more involved in a movement?

Further reading:

Colin Marshall and Tony Payne, *The Trellis and the Vine* (Kingsford, NSW, Australia: Matthias Media, 2009).

12 Glimpses of a Disciple-Making Community

1. When and where have you had a glimpse of a disciple-making community?

2. Can you describe a time when you have known you were in the throne room of God?

3. From Ephesians, what do you learn about Christ—and about your identity and birthright in Christ—that encourages you to more boldly and confidently approach God's throne of grace?

Notes

PREFACE

[1]Alan Hirsch, *The Forgotten Ways* (Grand Rapids: Brazos Press, 2006).

[2]Mike Cochrane, fellow disciple, and currently elder of the Warehouse Church in Aurora, IL.

INTRODUCTION

[1]On May 2, 2011, the Navy Seals captured and killed Osama bin Laden in the city of Abbottabad.

[2]This church would later become our home church, faithfully praying for us and supporting us for more than forty years.

[3]Robert N. Bellah et al., *Habits of the Heart: Individualism and Commitment in American Life* (New York: Harper & Row, 1985).

[4]Donald McGavran, *Understanding Church Growth* (Grand Rapids: Eerdmans, 1970).

[5]Ray Stedman, *Body Life* (Glendale, CA: Regal Books, 1972).

[6]Paul Little, *How to Give Away Your Faith* (Downers Grove, IL: InterVarsity Press, 1966).

[7]Paul Hiebert, "Beyond Anticolonialism to Globalism," in *Anthropological Reflections on Missiological Issues* (Grand Rapids: Baker Books, 1994), p. 55.

[8]Ibid., p. 59.

[9]Ibid., p. 64.

[10]When notes or lines of music get too close together it creates dissonance that demands to be resolved, thus creating movement forward.

1 WHAT IS A DISCIPLE ANYWAY?

[1]Alan Hirsch, *The Forgotten Ways* (Grand Rapids: Brazos Press, 2006), p. 41.

[2]Bill Hull, *The Disciple-Making Pastor* (Old Tappan, NJ: Revell, 1988), pp. 56-57.

[3]For more on categorization, see Paul Hiebert, "The Category *Christian* in

the Mission Task," in *Anthropological Reflections on Missiological Issues* (Grand Rapids: Baker Books, 1994).

[4]James 2:19.

[5]For more information on epistemology, see Paul Hiebert, "Reflections on Epistemological Foundations," in *Anthropological Reflections on Missiological Issues* (Grand Rapids: Baker Books, 1994).

[6]Philippians 3:13.

[7]Acts 18:10.

[8]John 21:15-18.

[9]Mike Breen, *Building a Discipleship Culture* (Pawleys Island, SC: 3 Dimension Ministries, 2011).

2 DISCIPLES LET GOD LEAD FROM THE INVISIBLE WORLD

[1]Names have been changed.

[2]Alan Hirsch dedicates a large section of his book *The Forgotten Ways* to the recovery of the principle.

[3]"*Sherlock Holmes* (2009 film)," Wikipedia, http://en.wikipedia.org/wiki/Sherlock_Holmes_(2009_film).

[4]Acts 26:9.

[5]Ruth Haley Barton, *Pursuing God's Will Together* (Downers Grove, IL: InterVarsity Press, 2012).

[6]Adele Ahlberg Calhoun, *Spiritual Disciplines Handbook: Practices That Transform Us* (Downers Grove, IL: InterVarsity Press), 2005.

[7]Matthew 26:53.

[8]2 Kings 6:16-17.

[9]Notes taken during a lecture given by Dr. Dudley Woodberry, professor at Fuller Theological Seminary, to workers assembled in Kabul, Afghanistan, 2006. Woodberry's findings contributed to the valuable work *From Seed to Fruit: Global Trends, Fruitful Practices, and Emerging Issues Among Muslims* (Pasadena, CA: William Carey Library, 2008).

[10]Paul Hiebert, "The Flaw of the Excluded Middle," in *Anthropological Reflections on Missiological Issues* (Grand Rapids: Baker Books, 1994), pp. 189-202.

3 DISCIPLES HEAR AND OBEY

[1]The sources for this summary of the life of Bakht Singh are a compilation from T. E. Koshy, *Bakht Sing of India* (Colorado Springs, CO: Authentic Publishing, 2008), and Daniel Smith, *Bakht Singh of India* (Washington, DC:

International Students Press, 1959). The current edition of the Koshy book is being produced by InterVarsity Press.

[2] Deuteronomy 10:19.

[3] Revelation 1:8.

[4] Revelation 21:6.

[5] Revelation 1:17.

[6] Isaiah 46:10.

[7] Ephesians 4:15-29.

[8] Paul Hiebert, *Anthropological Insights for Missionaries* (Grand Rapids: Baker Books, 1985), p. 46.

[9] I had the privilege of studying with Ted Ward during my doctoral studies at Trinity International University in 1990, and heard this statement.

[10] Isaiah 55:11.

[11] Tom Hovestol, *Extreme Righteousness: Seeing Ourselves in the Pharisees* (Chicago: Moody Press, 1997).

[12] See more at www.ignatianspirituality.com.

[13] See http://3dmovements.com/.

4 DISCIPLES DEVELOP RELATIONAL INTERDEPENDENCE

[1] Often attributed to Ken Blanchard, this saying may be Japanese in origin. See http://thinkexist.com/quotation/none_of_us_are_as_smart_as_all _of/160488.html.

[2] Colossians 1:15-20.

[3] Philippians 2:9-11.

[4] Larry Crabb, *Connecting* (Nashville: W Publishing Group, 1997), pp. 57, 60.

[5] Ruth Haley Barton, *Pursuing God's Will Together* (Downers Grove, IL: InterVarsity Press, 2012), p. 77.

[6] Geert Hofstede, *Culture's Consequences: International Differences in Work-Related Values* (Newbury Park, CA: Sage Publications, 1980), p. 11.

[7] Charles Davis, "Worldview of Middle-Class Small-Town and Urban Venezuelans with Perspectives on the Church" (PhD diss., Trinity Evangelical Divinity School, 1995).

[8] Michael Kearney, *World View* (Novato, CA: Chandler & Sharp, 1984).

[9] Bill Davidow, "The Internet 'Narcissim Epidemic,'" *The Atlantic*, March 26, 2013, www.theatlantic.com/health/archive/2013/03/the-internet-narcissism -epidemic/274336/.

[10]Robert N. Bellah et al., *Habits of the Heart: Individualism and Commitment in American Life* (New York: Harper & Row, 1985), p. 151.

[11]*"Que! ¿Es una visita médica?"*

[12]Hofstede, *Culture's Consequences*, p. 158.

[13]J. R. Katzenbach and D. K. Smith, *The Wisdom of Teams: Creating the High-Performance Organization* (Boston, MA: Harvard Business Press, 1992).

[14]Revelation 5:9-10.

5 DISCIPLES DO WHAT LOVE REQUIRES

[1]*The Manila Manifesto*, Section A.4, "The Gospel and Social Responsibility," www.lausanne.org/en/documents/manila-manifesto.html.

[2]John 4:1-26.

[3]Acts 2:14-41.

[4]Acts 16:16-34.

[5]Matthew 19:16-29.

[6]Matthew 8:5-13.

[7]Acts 8:26-40.

[8]Luke 24:13-35.

[9]Al Hsu has written an excellent article on this theme entitled, "A Multi-faceted Gospel: Why evangelicals shouldn't be threatened by new tellings of the good news," *Christianity Today*, April 10, 2008, www.christianitytoday .com/ct/2008/april/17.66.html.

[10]Luke 6:39-40.

[11]David J. Bosch, *Transforming Mission: Paradigm Shifts in Theology of Mission* (Maryknoll, NY: Orbis Books, 1991), p. 342.

[12]Stieg Larsson, *The Girl with the Dragon Tattoo* (New York: Random House, 2008). Reference to this book and the two that followed should not be construed as a recommendation by the author. The books are extremely dark and distressing.

[13]Peter Berger, Brigitte Berger and Hansfried Kellner, *The Homeless Mind* (New York: Random House, 1974), p. 9.

[14]Rodney Stark, *The Rise of Christianity* (San Francisco: HarperCollins, 1997), p. 75.

[15]Ibid., p. 161.

[16]Thomas Cahill, *How the Irish Saved Civilization* (New York: Doubleday, 1995).

[17]This material is drawn from reports by TEAM missionaries who participated in CHE training in Pakistan. More information can be found at Global CHE Network, www.chenetwork.org/.

[18]Matthew Paris, "As an atheist, I truly believe Africa needs God," *Times*, December 27, 2008.

[19]twitter.com/memphishalom.

[20]"The Shalom Project," Second Presbyterian Church, Memphis, TN, thesh alomproject.org/Upload/PDF/2010-shalom-report-full.pdf, p. 10.

6 Disciples Make Disciples

[1]Acts 2.

[2]Matthew 5–7.

[3]Acts 20.

[4]Matthew 13.

[5]John Stott, *Between Two Worlds* (Grand Rapids: Eerdmans, 1982).

[6]Edward T. Hall, *Beyond Culture* (Garden City, NY: Anchor Press/Doubleday, 1976), p. 76.

[7]Ibid., p. 79.

[8]Rodney Stark, *The Rise of Christianity* (San Francisco: HarperCollins, 1997), p. 18.

[9]In May of 2014 I had the privilege of attending the meetings of the Mission Commission of the World Evangelical Alliance. Jerry Trousdale of CityTeam and David Garrison of IMB presented a session on disciplemaking movements. Jerry Trousdale has written the book *Miraculous Movements* (Nashville, TN: Thomas Nelson, 2012), describing what is taking place in some of these movements.

[10]Steve Smith with Ying Kai, *T4T: A Discipleship Re-Revolution* (Monument, CO: WIGTake resources, 2011).

[11]Mike Breen, *Building a Discipleship Culture* (Pawleys Island, SC: 3 Dimension Ministries, 2011), p. 203.

[12]"Urban Population (% of total), The World Bank, http://data.worldbank .org/indicator/SP.URB.TOTL.IN.ZS?page=6.

[13]William J. Smole, *World Book Encyclopedia*, "Venezuela" (Chicago: World Book, 1990), p. 317.

[14]See New Life Community Church, www.newlifechicago.org.

7 LEADERS EQUIP DISCIPLES FOR MINISTRY

[1]Roland Allen, *Missionary Methods: St. Paul's or Ours?* (Grand Rapids: Eerdmans, 1962), p. 81. [First published in 1912.]

[2]Alan Hirsch and Tim Catchim, *The Permanent Revolution* (San Francisco: Jossey-Bass, 2012).

[3]Mike Breen and Steve Cockram, *Building a Discipleship Culture* (Pawleys Island, SC: 3 Dimension Ministries, 2011).

[4]Romans 12, 1 Corinthians 12 and Ephesians 4.

[5]Matthew 20:20-28.

[6]Heard and recorded in a seminar with Alan Hirsch in Paris, France, April 2011.

[7]A presentation by Dale Anderson, musician and TEAM missionary to France, in a seminar during a church planting school sponsored by TEAM in the mid-'90s.

[8]James E. Plueddemann, *Leading Across Cultures: Effective Ministry and Mission in the Global Church* (Downers Grove, IL: InterVarsity Press, 2009).

[9]www.ccl.org/leadership/pdf/assessments/GlobeStudy.pdf.

[10]David Garrison, *Church Planting Movements: How God Is Redeeming a Lost World* (Monument, CO: WIGTake Resources, 2004).

[11]Conversation with Robert Lopez, Filipino mission leader, during a triennial conference of the Mission Commission in Germany, 2011.

[12]Global Missiology, http://ojs.globalmissiology.org/index.php/english /article/viewFile/118/340.

8 DISCIPLES LIVE AN UNDIVIDED LIFE

[1]Matthew 13:55-56.

[2]Herodians had a political agenda and were favorable toward Rome; they had the secular slider switch set high.

[3]Pharisees wanted religion to control all of life; they had the sacred slider switch set extremely high.

[4]Ephesians 6:5-9.

[5]Psalm 146.

[6]Michael Kearney, *World View* (Novato, CA: Chandler & Sharp, 1984).

[7]Paul Hiebert, *Anthropological Reflections on Missiological Issues* (Grand Rapids: Baker Books, 1994), p. 112.

[8]Ibid., pp. 110-11.

[9]Dorothy L. Sayers, *The Mind of the Maker* (San Francisco: Harper, 1941).

[10]Steve Rundle and Tom Steffens, *Great Commission Companies* (Downers Grove, IL: InterVarsity Press, 2003).

[11]Sean, Irish pastor and leader of the evangelical community of Ireland, spoke at a conference of TEAM missionaries in 1996 at which I was present.

9 DISCIPLES ENGAGE IN PERSONAL AND CULTURAL TRANSFORMATION

[1]Jerry Bridges, *Respectable Sins* (Colorado Springs, CO: NavPress, 2007).

[2]Roger Crowley, *Constantinople: The Last Great Siege, 1453* (London: Faber and Faber Limited Bloomsbury House, 2005).

[3]Philemon 1-25.

[4]Duane Elmer, *Cross-Cultural Conflict* (Downers Grove, IL: InterVarsity Press, 1993).

[5]Duane Elmer, *Cross-Cultural Connections* (Downers Grove, IL: InterVarsity Press, 2002).

[6]Charles Davis, "Worldview of Middle-Class Small-Town and Urban Venezuelans with Perspectives on the Church" (PhD diss., Trinity Evangelical Divinity School, 1995), p. 209.

[7]Shirl James Hoffman, "Sports Fanatics," *Christianity Today*, January 29, 2010, www.christianitytoday.com/ct/2010/february/sports-fanatics-football -shirl-hoffman.html?start=4.

[8]Heard during a consultation with a church.

[9]In 2006 I interviewed a retired missionary who, shortly after his arrival in Papua in the 1950s, had seen men from one tribe rowing downriver in their canoes, carrying body parts for a feast. They had just raided another village, where they killed, dismembered and gathered food for their feast.

[10]Don Richardson, *Peace Child* (Ventura, CA: Regal Books, 2005).

[11]Richardson coined the term "redemptive analogy" to describe this process.

[12]The video *Never the Same*, describing their journey, is available at http:// vimeo.com/51281742.

[13]Albert Y. Hsu, *The Suburban Christian* (Downers Grove, IL: InterVarsity Press, 2006).

10 DISCIPLES KEEP THE END IN MIND

[1]J. R .R. Tolkien, *The Lord of the Rings* (New York: Ballantine Books, 1954).

[2]Mark Buchanan, *The Rest of God* (Nashville: W Publishing Group, 2006), p. 125.

[3]William Easterly, *The White Man's Burden* (New York: Penguin Group, 2006), p. 11. "Sixty years of countless reform schemes to aid agencies and dozens of different plans, and $2.3 trillion later, the aid industry is still failing to reach the beautiful goal. The evidence points to an unpopular conclusion: Big Plans will always fail to reach the beautiful goal."

[4]Hugh Halter and Matt Smay, *The Tangible Kingdom* (San Francisco: Jossey-Bass, 2008).

[5]Vinoth Ramachandra, *Gods That Fail* (Downers Grove, IL: InterVarsity Press, 1996).

[6]Scot McKnight, *The Jesus Creed: Loving God, Loving Others* (Brewster, MA: Paraclete Press, 2004).

[7]Dallas Willard and Gary Black, *The Divine Conspiracy Continued: Fulfilling God's Kingdom on Earth* (New York: HarperCollins, 2014).

[8]Ephesians 1:20-22.

[9]Email correspondence between the author and TEAM missionary Keith McCune.

[10]E. Stanley Jones, *The Unshakable Kingdom and the Unchanging Person* (Nashville: Abingdon Press, 1972), pp. 30-31.

[11]Lucy Maud Montgomery, *Anne of Green Gables* (Boston: L. C. Page & Co., 1908).

[12]Insight derived from a lecture given by Dr. Paul Hiebert during courses taken at Trinity International Divinity School, 1990.

[13]Paul Sparks, Tim Soerens and Dwight J. Friesen, *The New Parish* (Downers Grove, IL: InterVarsity Press, 2014).

[14]Heard during an evangelical Anglican church service in Wheaton, IL, 2013.

[15]Notes from a lecture given at Trinity International University as part of the Carl F. Henry Lecture series, on October 27, 2010.

[16]Desmond Tutu, *Desmond Tutu: No Future Without Forgiveness* (New York: Doubleday, 1999).

[17]Cathleen Lawler, *Church Collaboration for City Transformation in a Context of Affluence: A Dissertation Submitted to the Faculty in Candidacy of the Degree of Doctor of Ministry* (Seattle: Bakke Graduate University, 2012), p. 123.

11 Disciples Organize Flexibly and Purposefully

[1]Gordon MacKenzie, *Orbiting the Giant Hairball: A Corporate Fool's Guide to Surviving with Grace* (New York: Viking Penguin, 1998).

[2]Alan Hirsch, *The Forgotten Ways* (Grand Rapids: Brazos Press, 2006), p. 179.

[3]Ibid., p. 182.

[4]Jerry Trousdale, in a session on disciple-making movements at the 2014 Mission Commission meetings of the WEA, said that of sixty-two movements they were studying, only one or two were in urban areas, and none in individualist countries.

[5]Notes taken during a lecture given by Dr. Dudley Woodbury, Fuller professor, to workers assembled in Kabul, Afghanistan, ca. 2006. Woodbury's findings contributed to the valuable work *From Seed to Fruit: Global Trends, Fruitful Practices, and Emerging Issues Among Muslims* (Pasadena, CA: William Carey Library, 2008).

12 GLIMPSES OF A DISCIPLE-MAKING COMMUNITY

[1]2 Corinthians 12:3-4.

[2]Ezekiel 1:25-28.

[3]Isaiah 6:1-4.

[4]Revelation 1:12-16.

[5]Ephesians 2:6.

About the Author

Dr. Charles Davis was raised for sixteen years in Pakistan by American parents. Later, he and his wife, Kris, lived and worked for twenty years in Venezuela where they raised their three children. While in Venezuela he did his field research for a PhD, studying Venezuelan worldview, the assumptions that everyday people make about life. More recently, his assignment as the director of TEAM, a global nonprofit agency, took him to thirty-five countries. Now he continues to apply a lifetime of insights to the fields of education, mission and the church, helping people learn to enjoy and benefit from the richness of global diversity. Find more at sliderswitches.com or search for Charles Davis on LinkedIn.

SliderSwitches is a consultancy set up to help people and organizations develop cultural competencies, based on the metaphor of a mixer board that balances the various "microphones" that together deliver cultural music. Visit sliderswitches.com or contact the author at sliderswitches@gmail.com.

Index